Copywright
Text and Images
All Rights Reserved

Gary Walters
2018

ISBN   978-1986902311

VECTOR PRINT AND PUBLISHING

BOUQUETS

WANDERING ALONG THE ROADSIDE I WOULD OFTEN STOP TO LOOK MORE CLOSELY AT SOME PLANT OR FLOWER OR BABY TREE OR ANCIENT TREE OR A ROCK OR BARK OR LICHEN. OFTEN, INDEED, MORE AND MORE OFTEN, I WOULD FIND DETRITUS HERE AND THERE. PAPER BAGS, PLASTIC BAGS, PAPER COFFEE CUPS, NEWSPRINT, BOTTLES, BOTTLE CAPS, STRING.
MANY OBJECTS THAT DIDN'T BELONG ON A ROAD THROUGH A FOREST, OR BESIDE THE STREAM THAT RAN THROUGH IT.

THIS WAS RICHARDSON ROAD AND WE HAD MOVED TO WHAT WAS PERHAPS THE FIRST FARM HOUSE IN THIS NECK OF THE WOODS. THE HOUSE WAS BUILT IN 1894. IT WAS SURROUNDED EVENTUALLY BY APPLE TREES. THE LAND SLOPED DOWN TO A SMALL LAKE, LAMEY LAKE, WHCH WAS PART OF THE WETLAND COMPLEX THAT LAY IN

ALL THE HOLLOWS CREATED BY THE GLACIERS WHEN THEY RETREATED. THIS COMPLEX AND THE PATH THAT WAS TO BECOME RICHARDSON ROAD WAS USED AS PART OF A PORTAGE BY THE INDIGENOUS PEOPLES FOR YEARS BEFORE THE ARRIVAL OF THE WHITE SETTLERS.

IT IS SAID THAT SAMUEL DE CHAMPLAIN, THE GREAT FRENCH EXPLORER, ALSO USED THIS PORTAGE. NOT TOO FAR AWAY THERE WAS AN IROQUOIS SETTLEMENT. WE ARE REMINDED THAT THE COMBINATION OF HUNTING AND SETTLED AGRICULTURE, AS WELL AS HARVESTS OF WILD RICE FROM RICE LAKE FURTHER SOUTH, SUPPLIED THE EARLIEST INHABITANTS WITH PLENTY OF FOOD.

SO WALKING ALONG THE ROAD WAS NOT ONLY TO LOOK AT THE CHANGING LANDSCAPE AND FOREST, IT WAS ALSO TO TO RUMINATE AND TO PEOPLE THE ROAD WITH FIGURES FROM THE DISTANT, THE VERY DISTANT PAST, AS WELL AS THE PRESENT.

THE ROAD HAS NOW RECEIVED A HERITAGE DESIGNATION. THE LAND ONCE INTACT IS DIVIDED

INTO LOTS WITH HOUSES AND GARDENS. THERE ARE MANY OLD APPLE TREES FROM THE ORIGINAL PLANTING. THERE ARE LONG LINES OF GATHERED STONE FROM THE PLOWING AND MAKING OF FIELDS. BUT THE ORIGINAL SETTLERS ARE GONE ALTHOUGH THERE IS A SO CALLED RESERVATION FURTHER SOUTH SELLING CIGARETTES, SOUVENIRS, MARIJUANA PRODUCTS, CAMPING EQUIPMENT, USED CARS, PLASTIC INFLATABLE DINOSAURS, CANOES, KAYAKS, FIREWOOD, FOOD AND DRINK. FOR THE HIGHWAY, #45, LEADS NOT ONLY TO THE TOWN OF HASTINGS BUT TO COTTAGE COUNTRY.

WE LIVED ON RICHARDSON ROAD FOR 15 YEARS. WE RESTORED MANY APPLE TREES, DUG OUT THE SUMAC IN ORDER TO MAKE GARDENS, AND HAD FINE LAWNS, A COUPLE OF FOUNTAINS, AND SCULPTURE WE BROUGHT BACK FROM OUR ANNUAL TRIPS TO BALI.

IRONICALLY THEN, THE NATIVE LANDSCAPE, HERE AS ELSEWHERE IN IN NORTH AND SOUTH AMERICA WAS TRANSFORMED INTO LAND MORE PROFITABLE IN SOME WAYS, BUT ALSO MORE TAME.

I HAVE WRITTEN ABOUT THIS TRANSFORMATION AND OUR LIFE THERE ELSEWHERE. THERE IS ALSO A BOOK OF PASTEL DRAWINGS OF THE RATHER UNIQUE AND LOVELY LANDSCAPE WE LIVED IN.

BUT THIS COLLECTION IS OF THE SMALL STUFF THAT CAME TO MY NOTICE. I WOULD BRING BACK LITTLE WILDFLOWER BOUQUETS, A ROCK OR TWO, MOSS (I ALSO MADE A BOOK ABOUT THE MOSS THEREABOUTS), INTERESTING BITS AND AND PIECES, AS WELL AS THE DETRITUS THAT WAS BEFOULING THE MARGINS OF THE WOODS, THAT WAS CREEPING AND BEING BLOWN FURTHER AND FURTHER INTO THE WOODS.

I WOULD MAKE A COMPOSITION OF THESE ELEMENTS ON MY SCANNER PLATE. I OFTEN ADDED FABRICS OR OTHER ELEMENTS THAT MIGHT SUGGEST THAT PLANTS CAN SPEAK AND HEAR EACH OTHER OR THAT THEY ARE PART OF PHILOSOPHY AND IDEAS AND, OF COURSE, VICE VERSA.

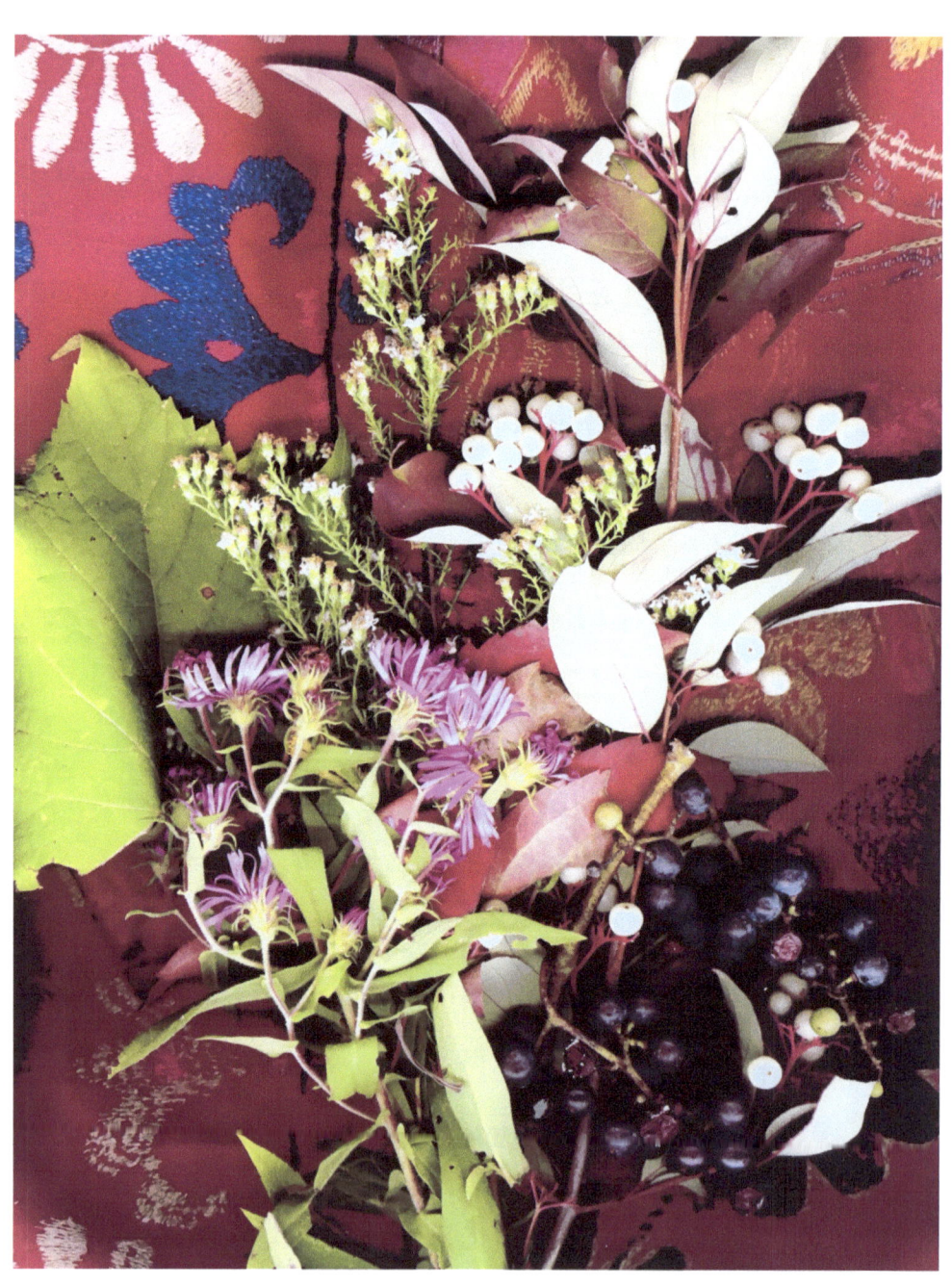

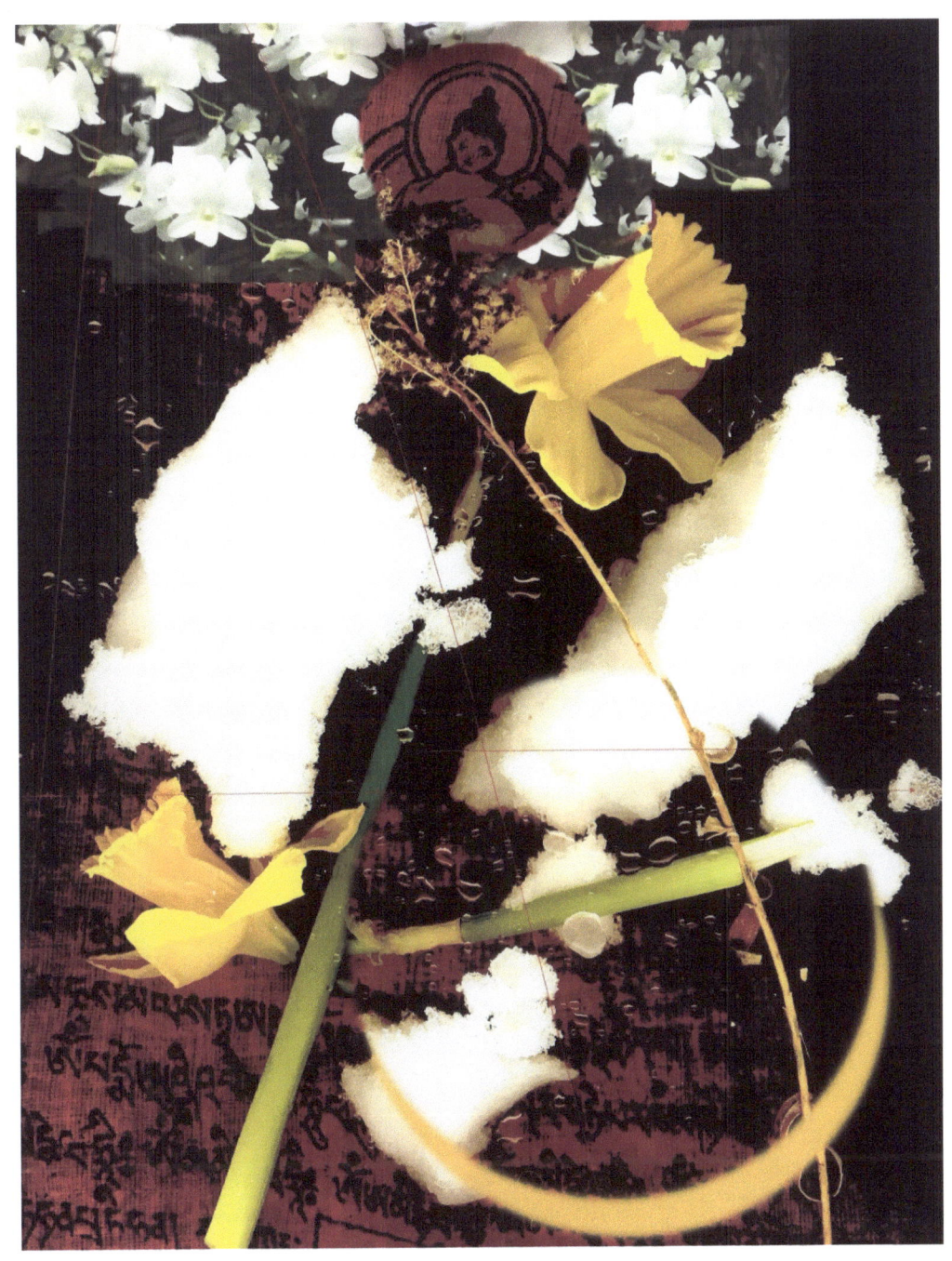

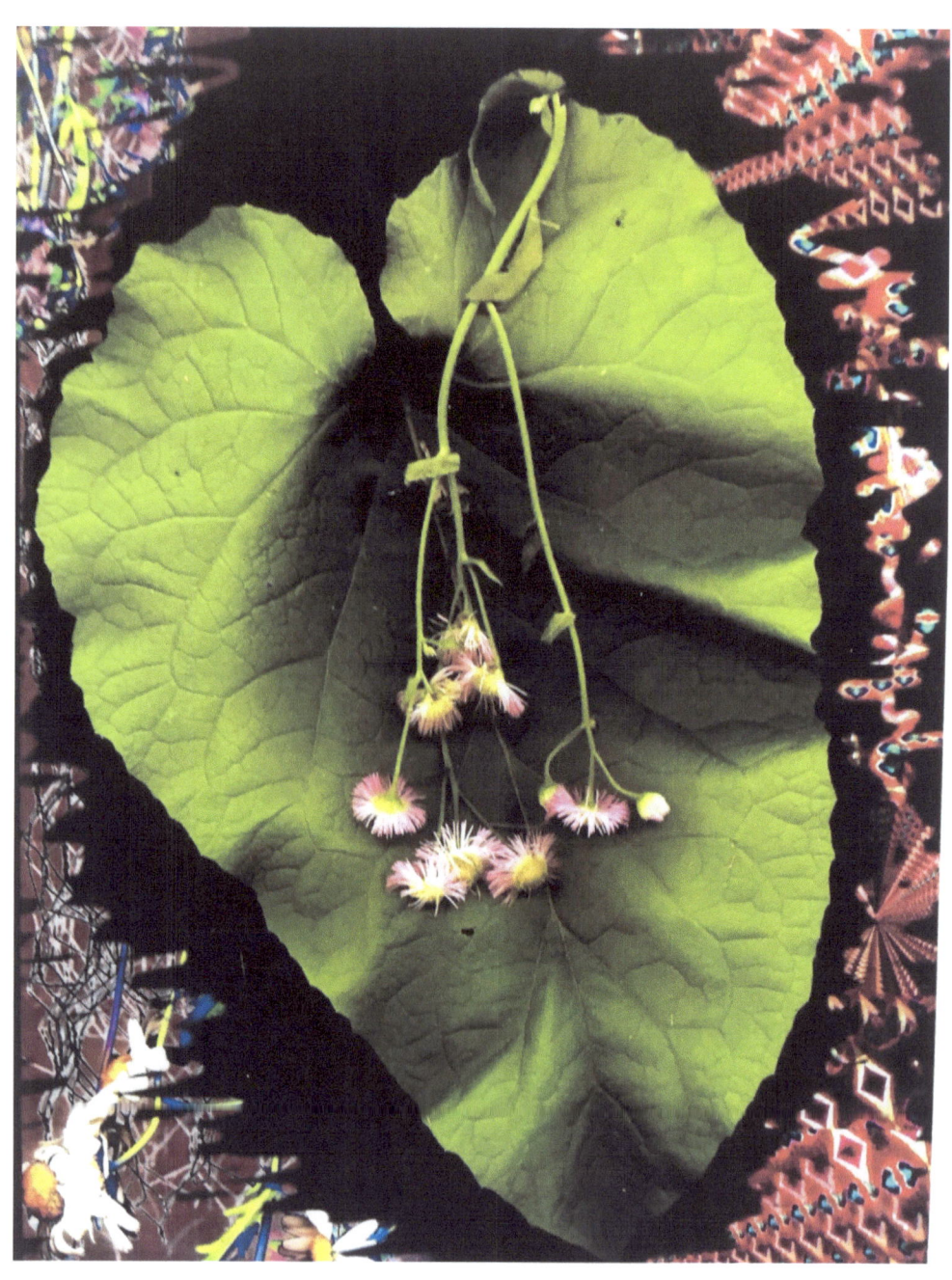

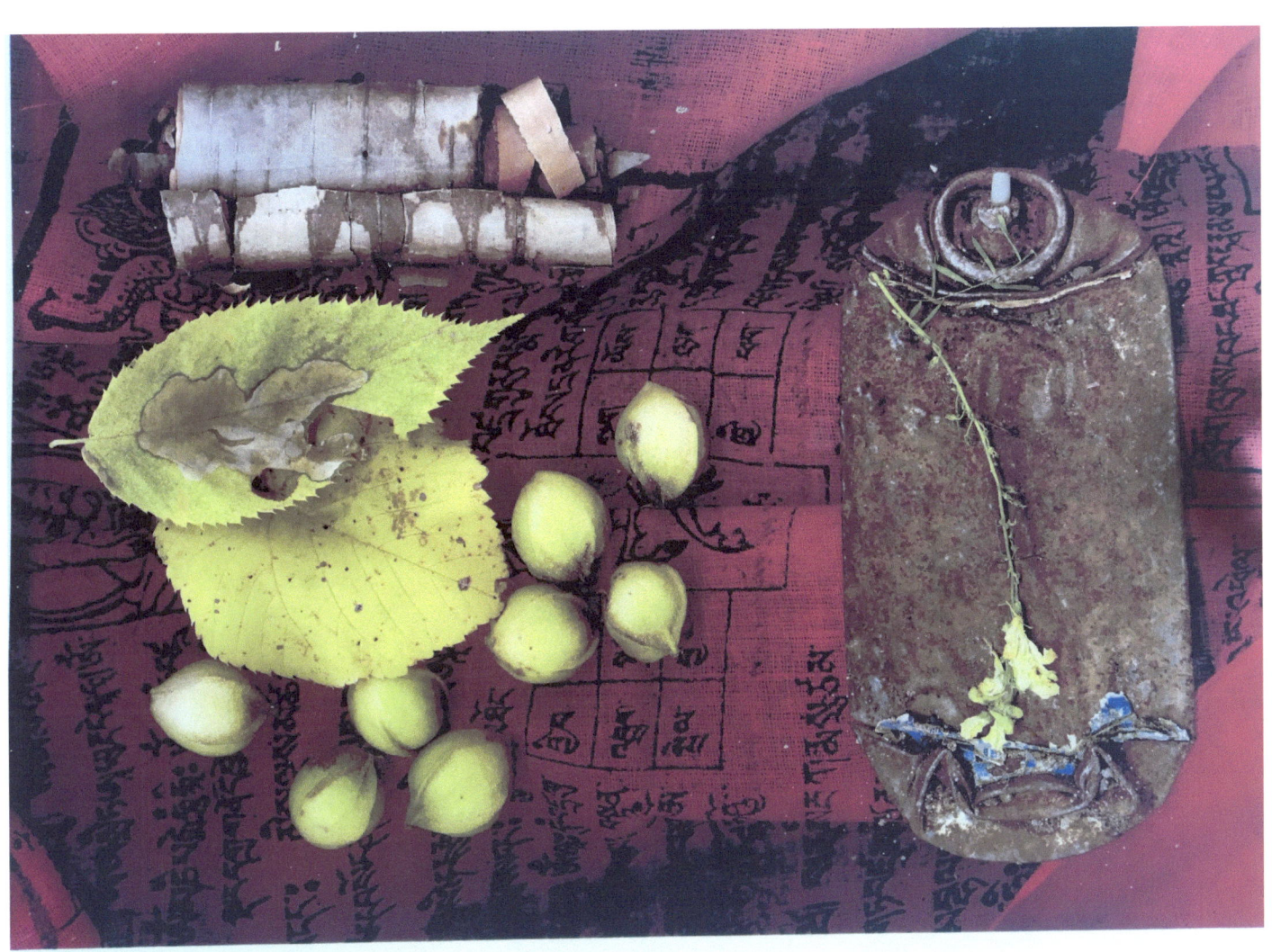

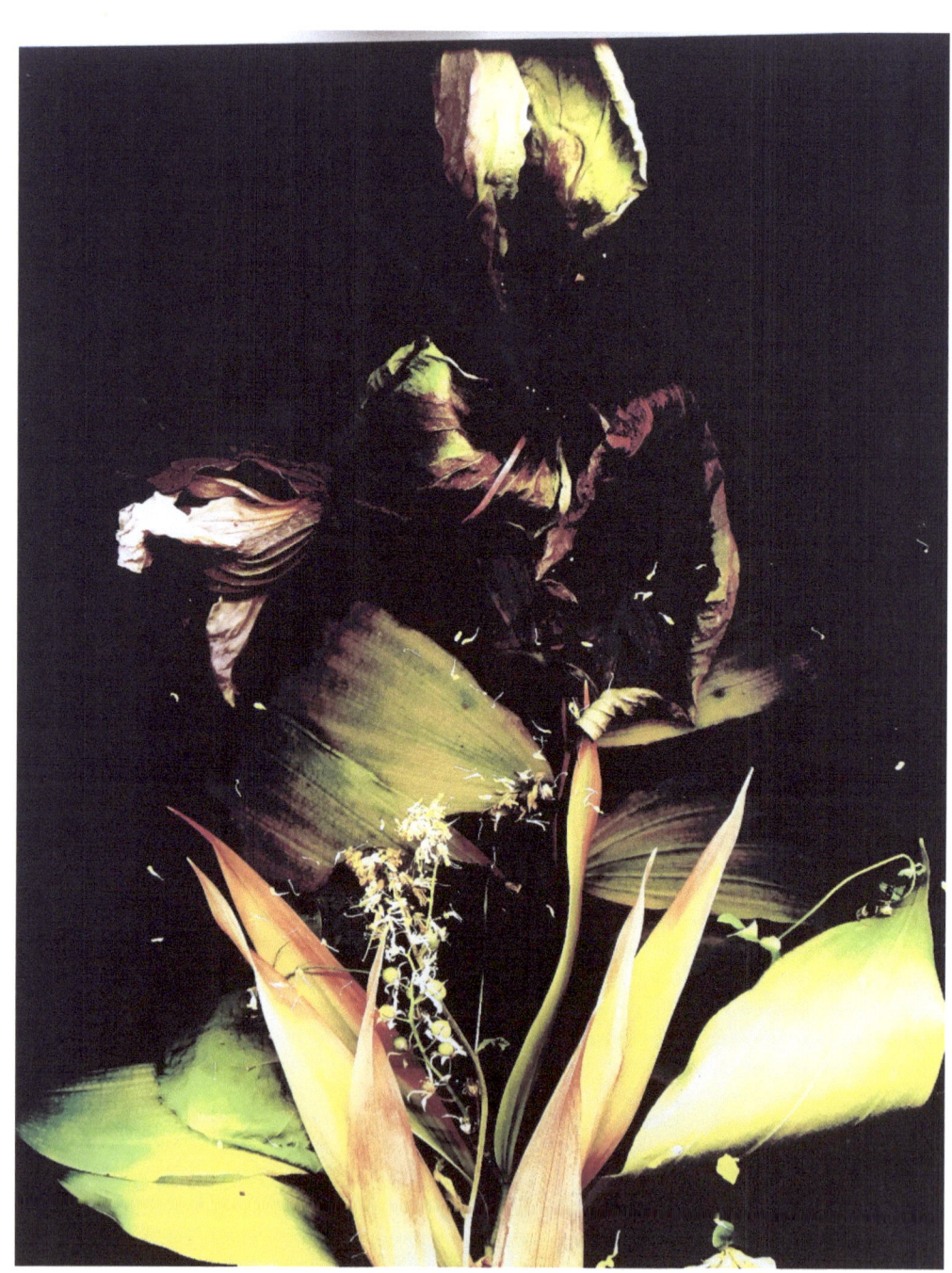

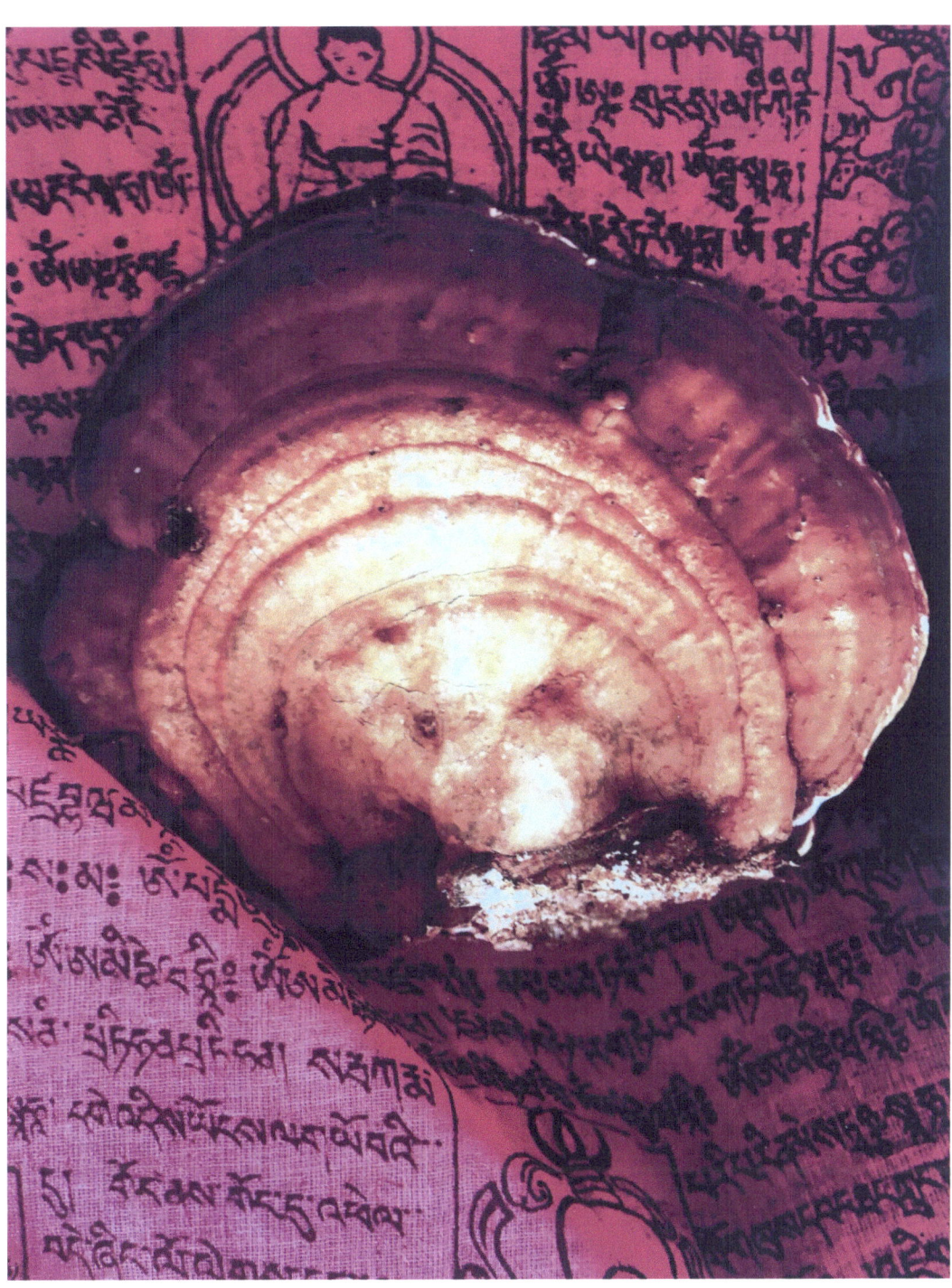

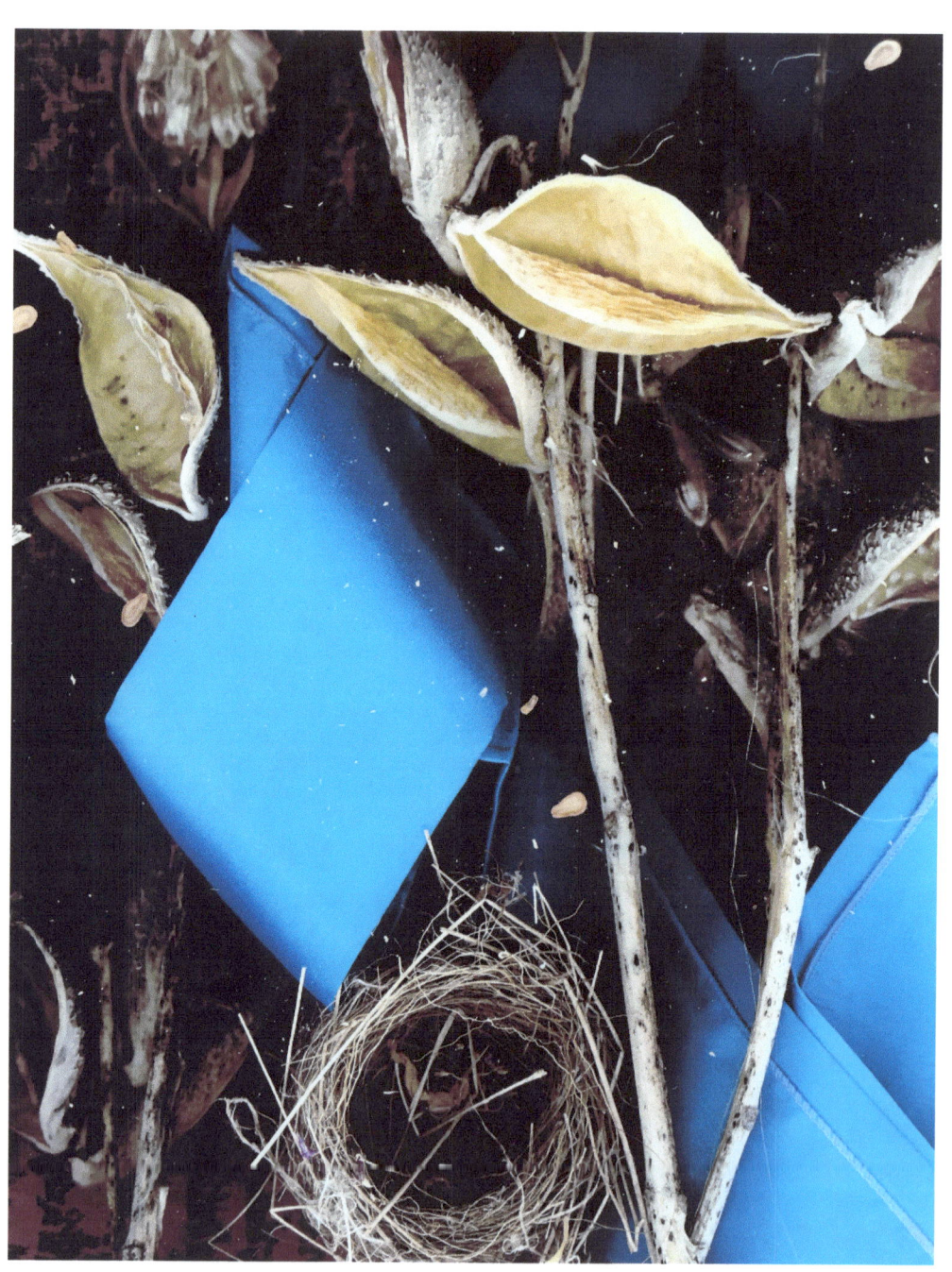

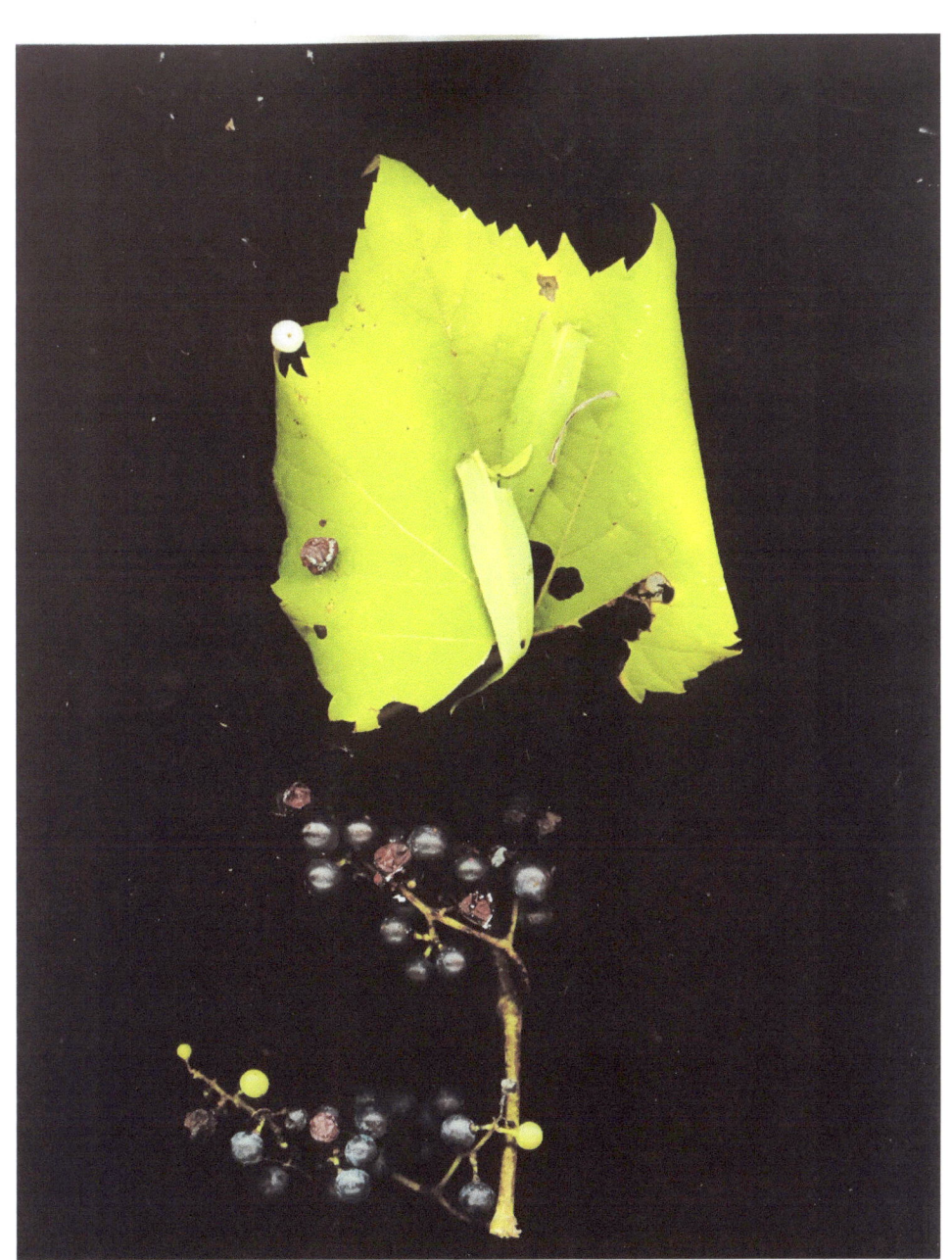

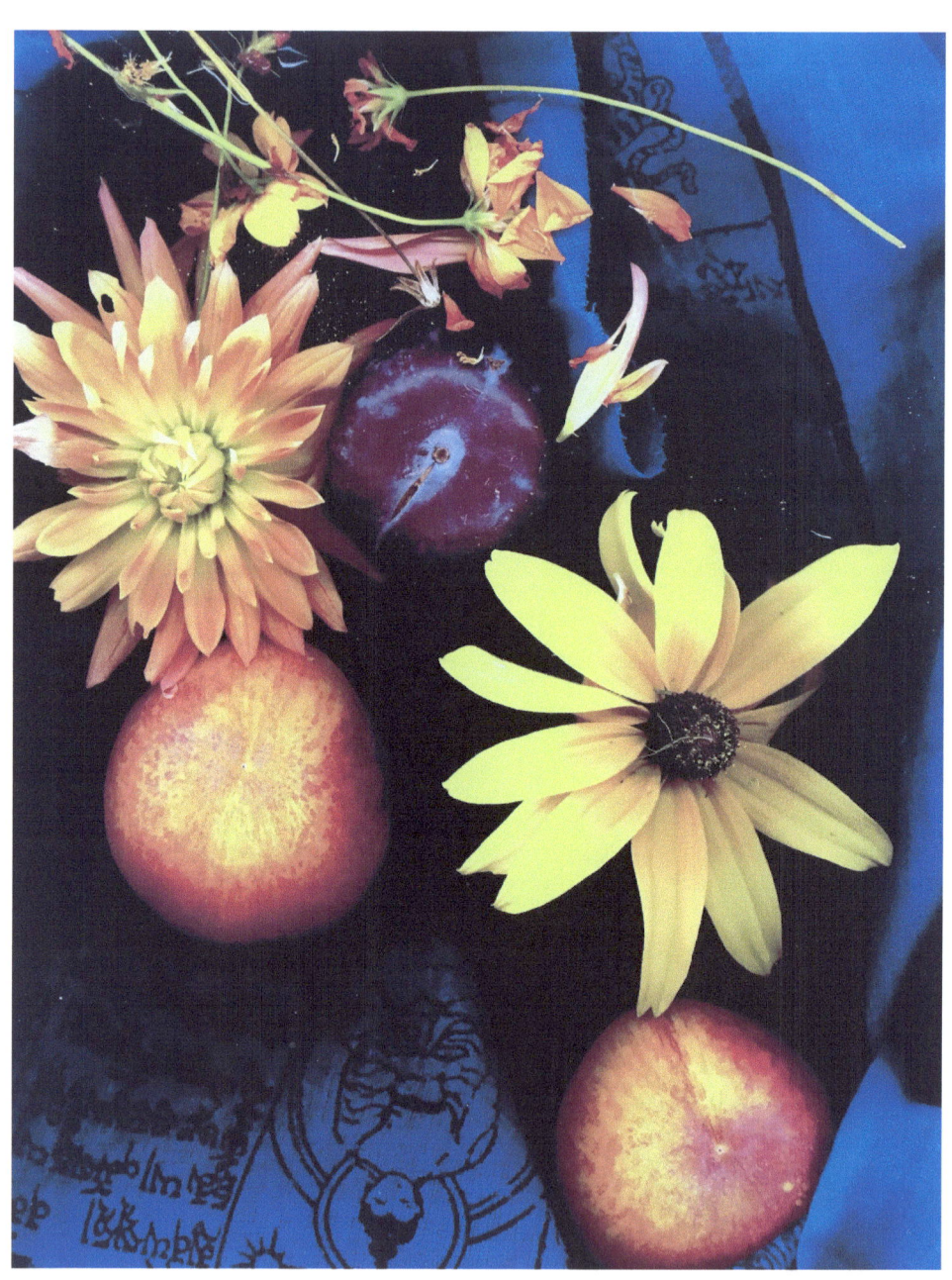

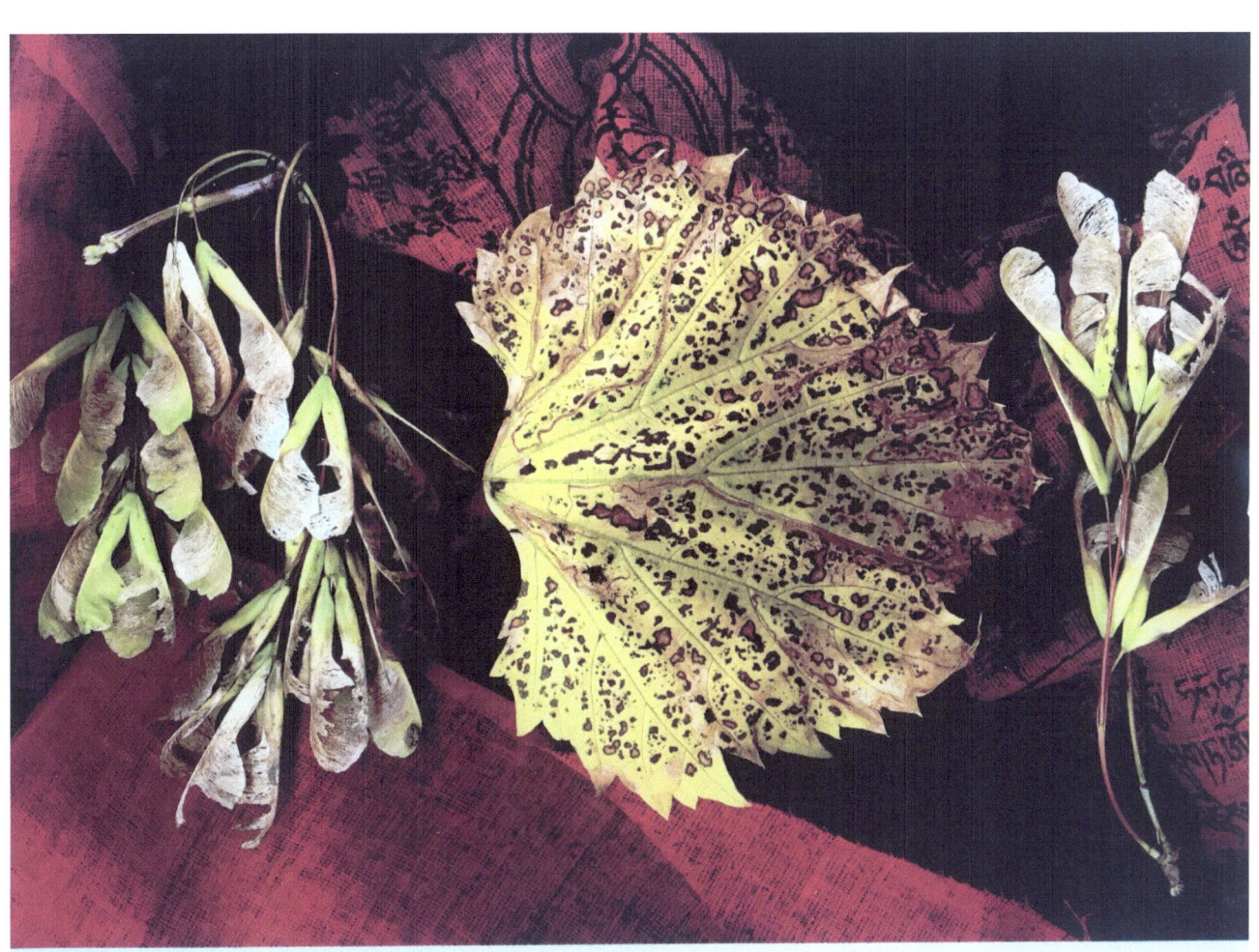

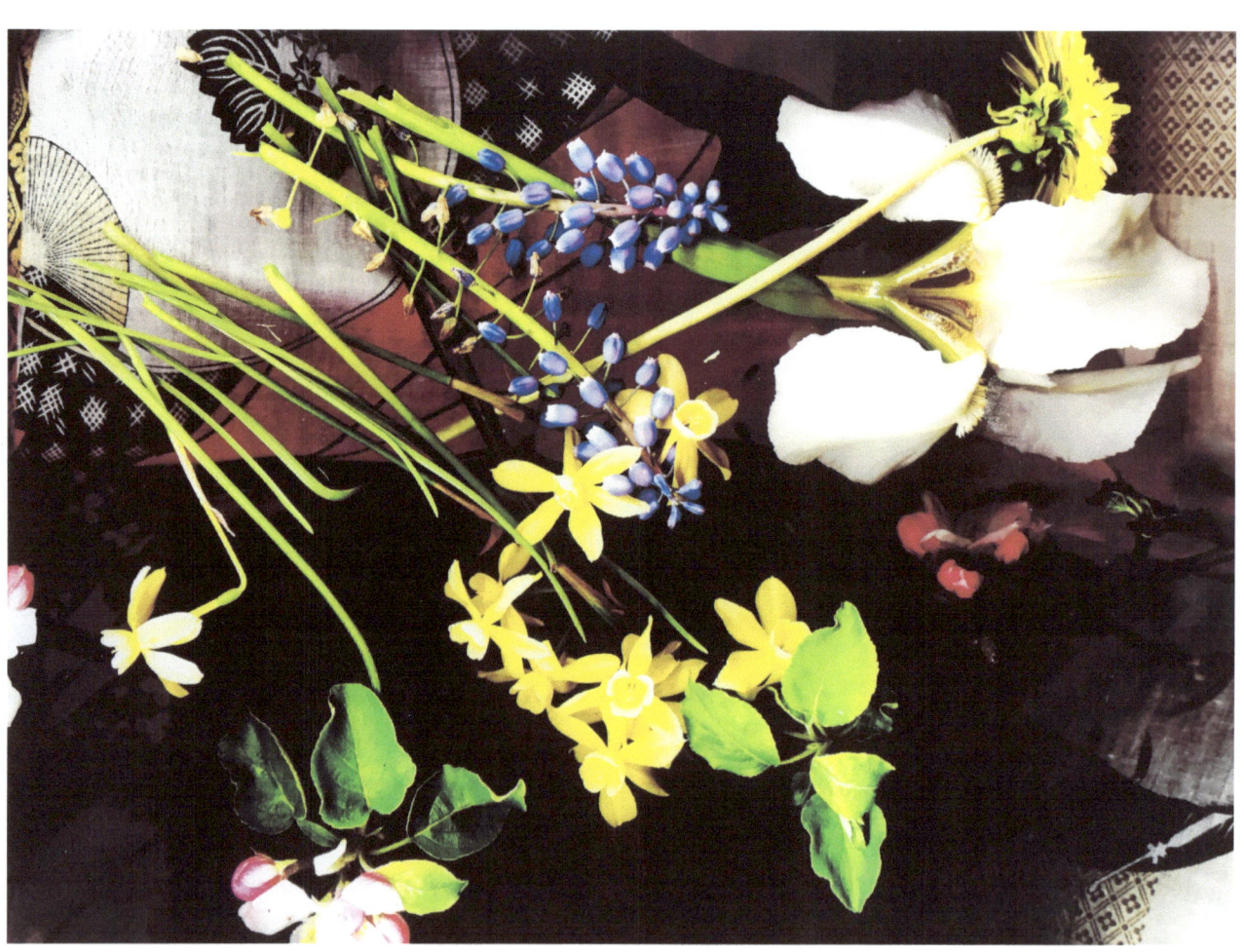

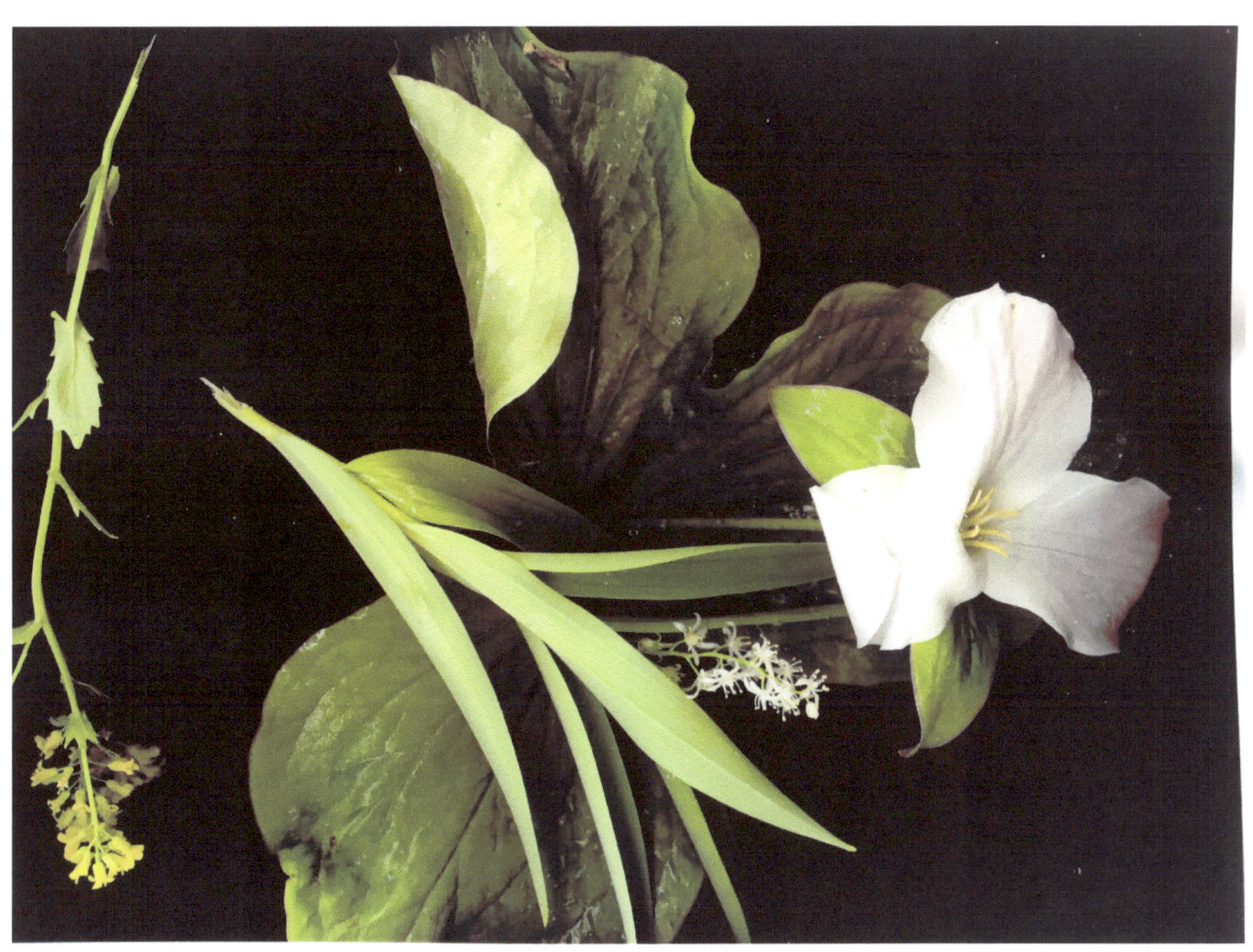

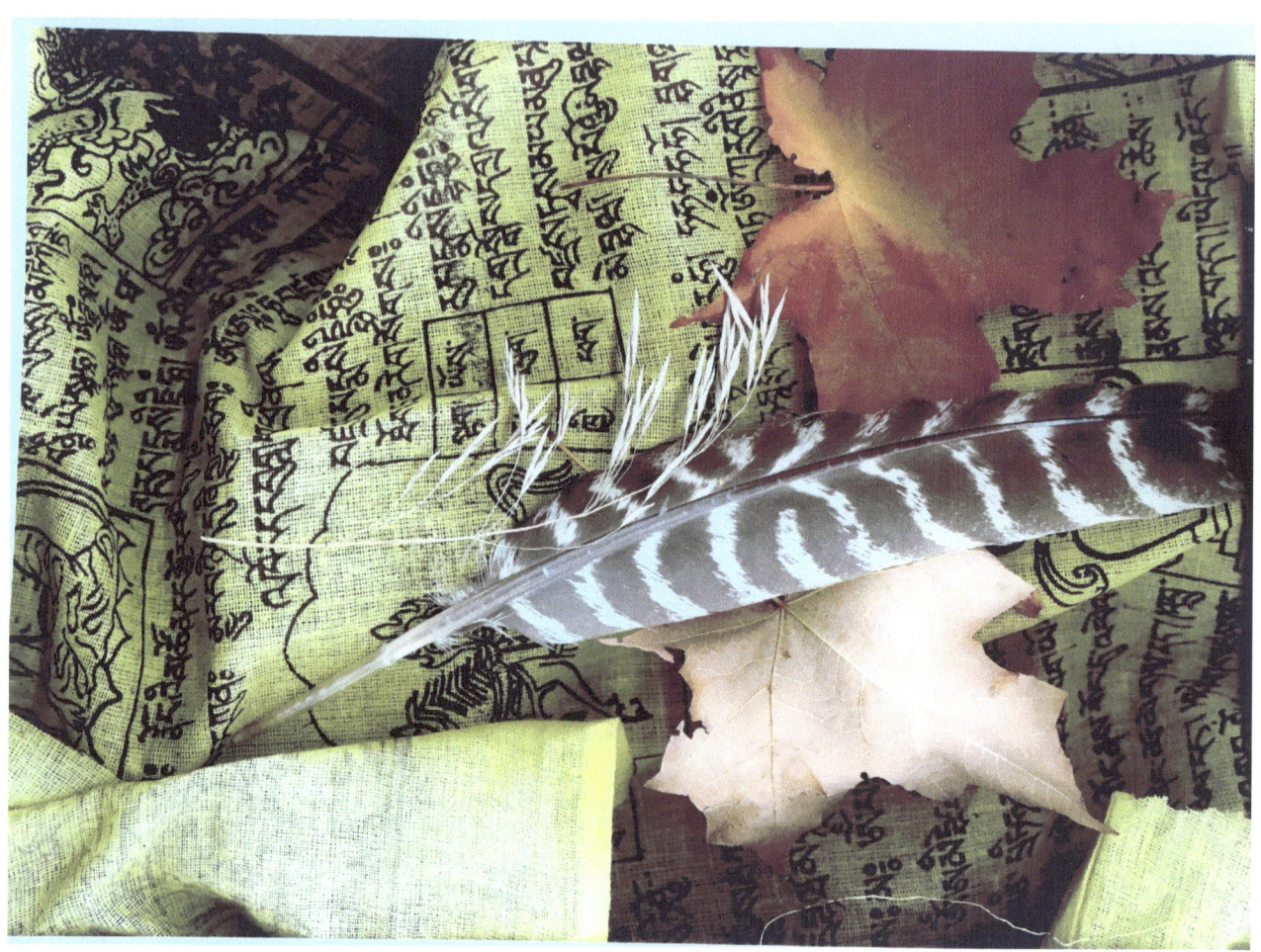

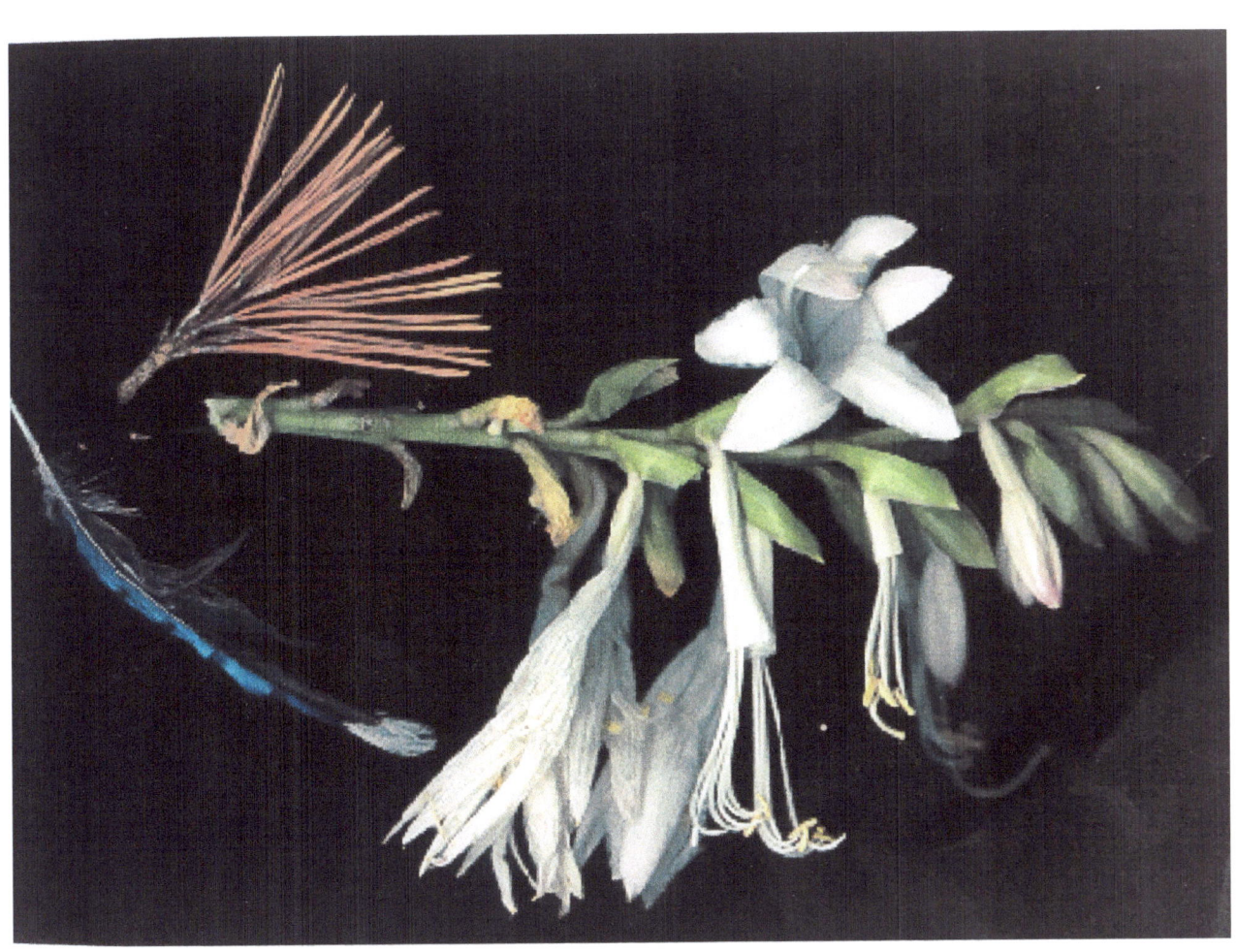

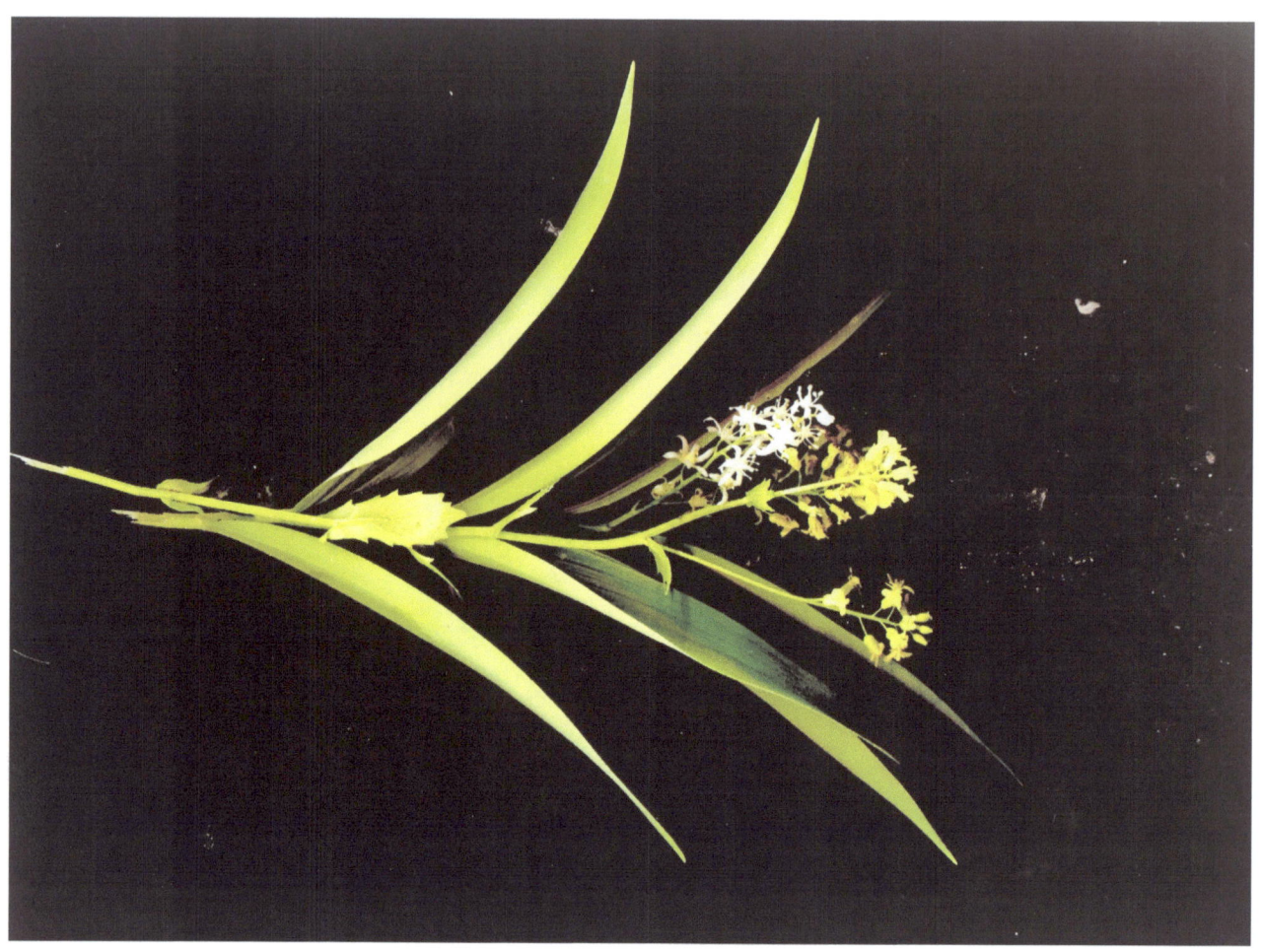

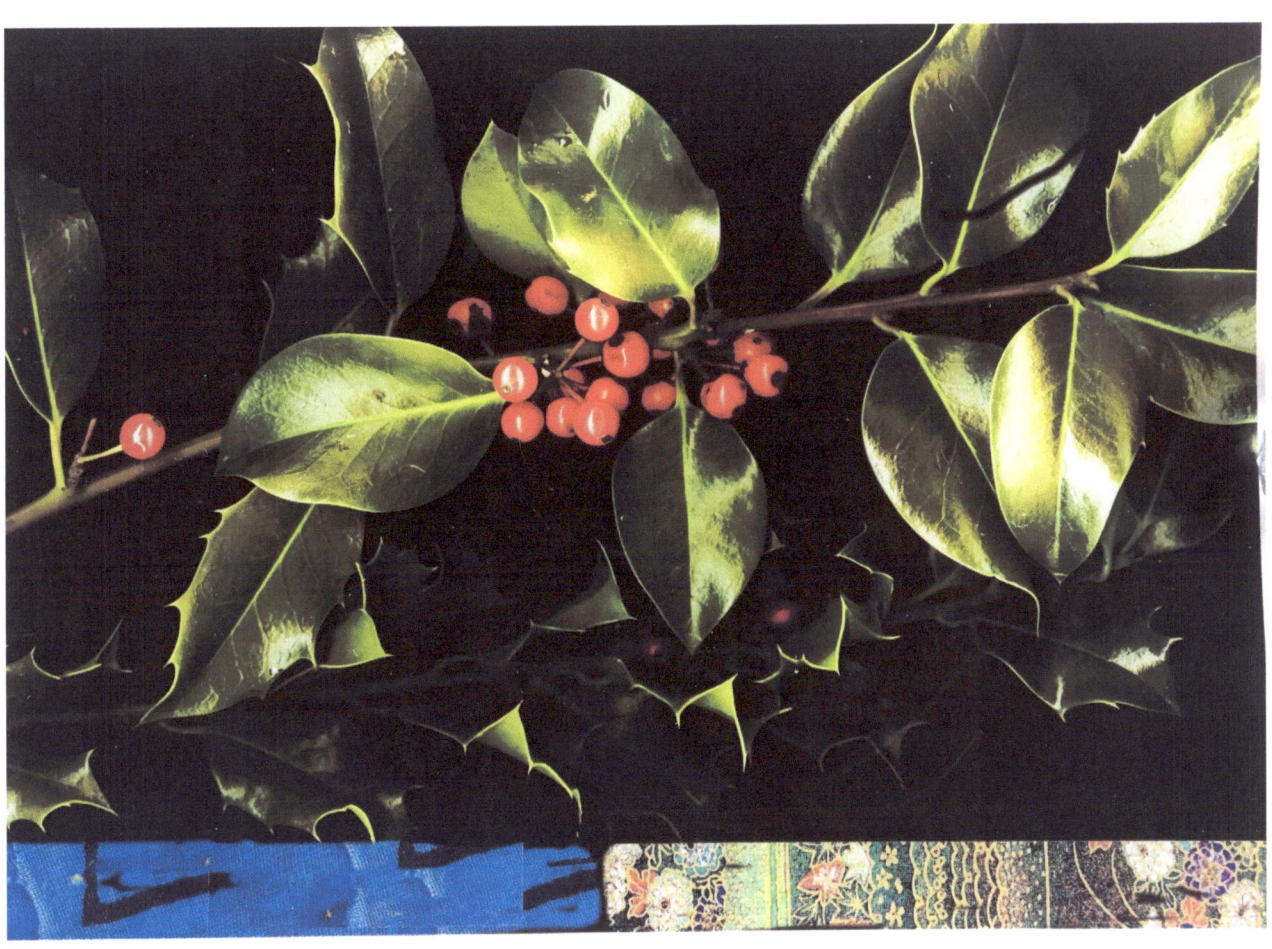

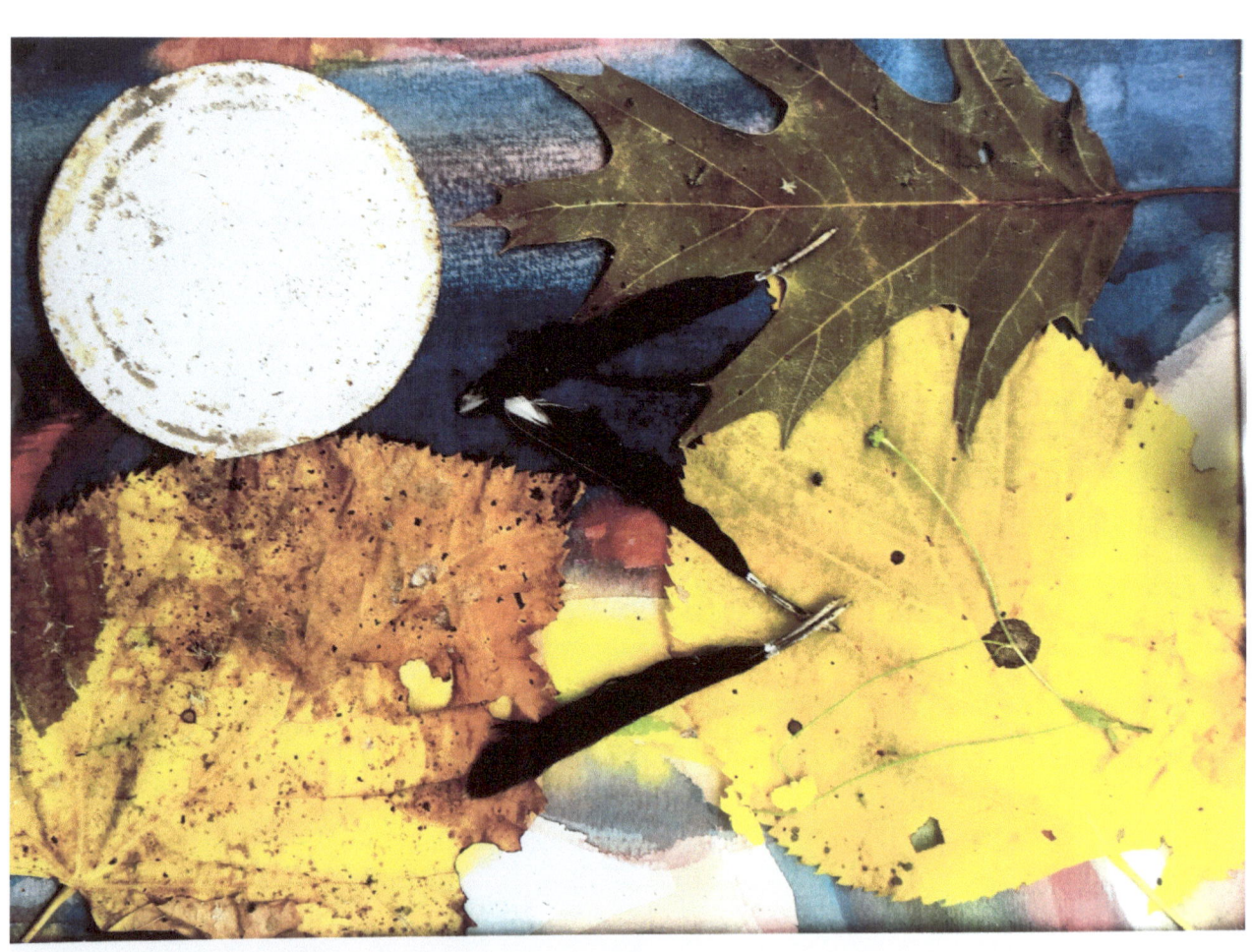

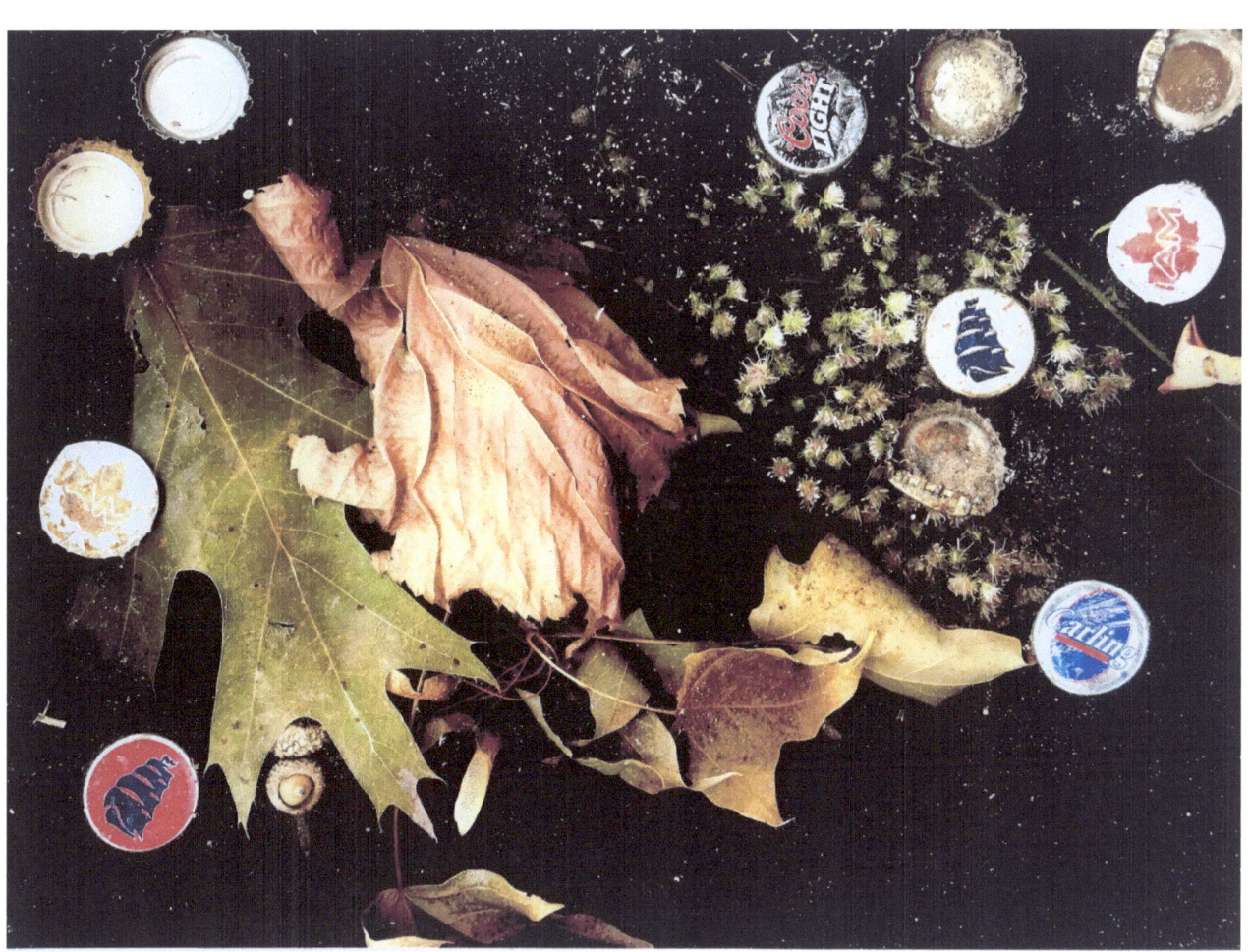

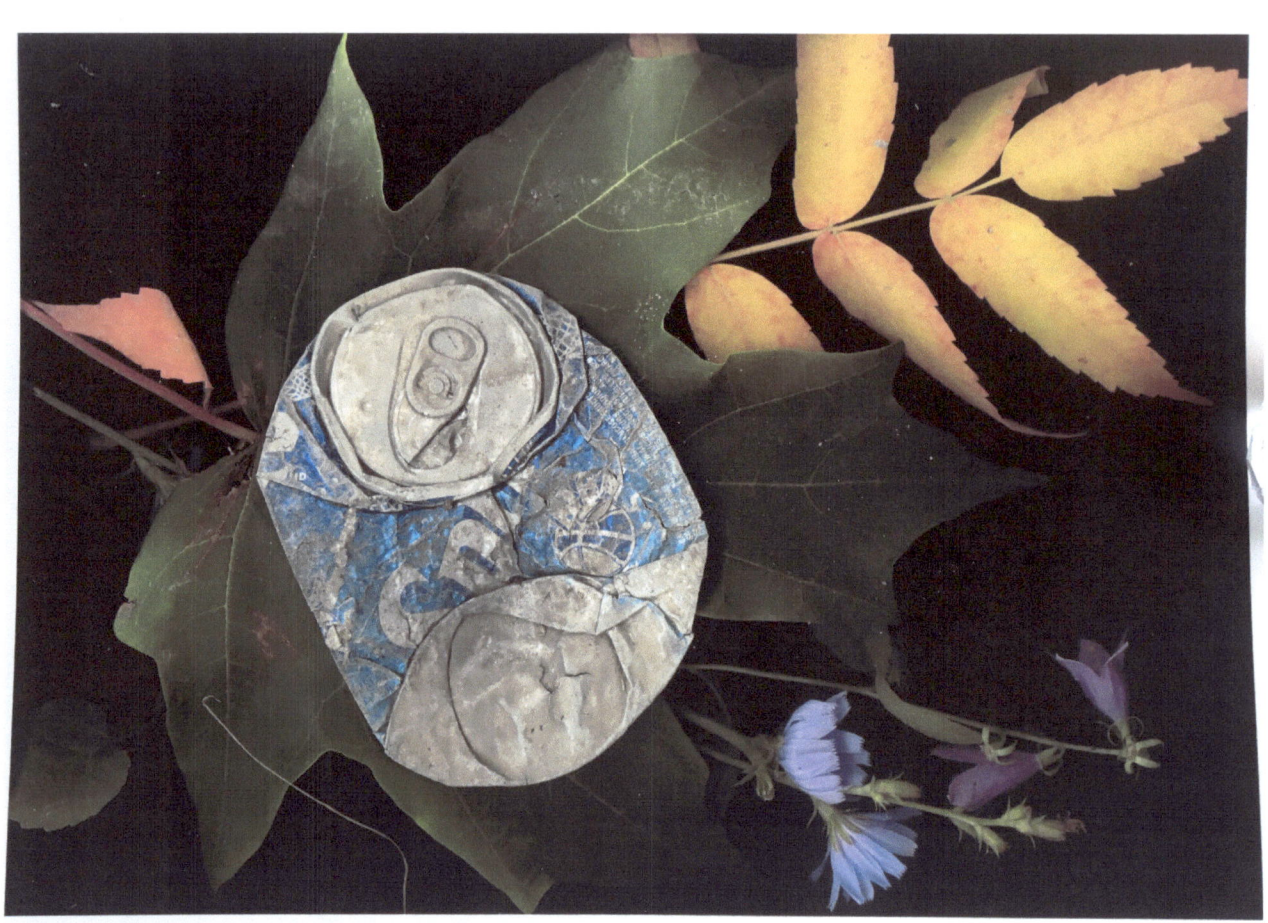

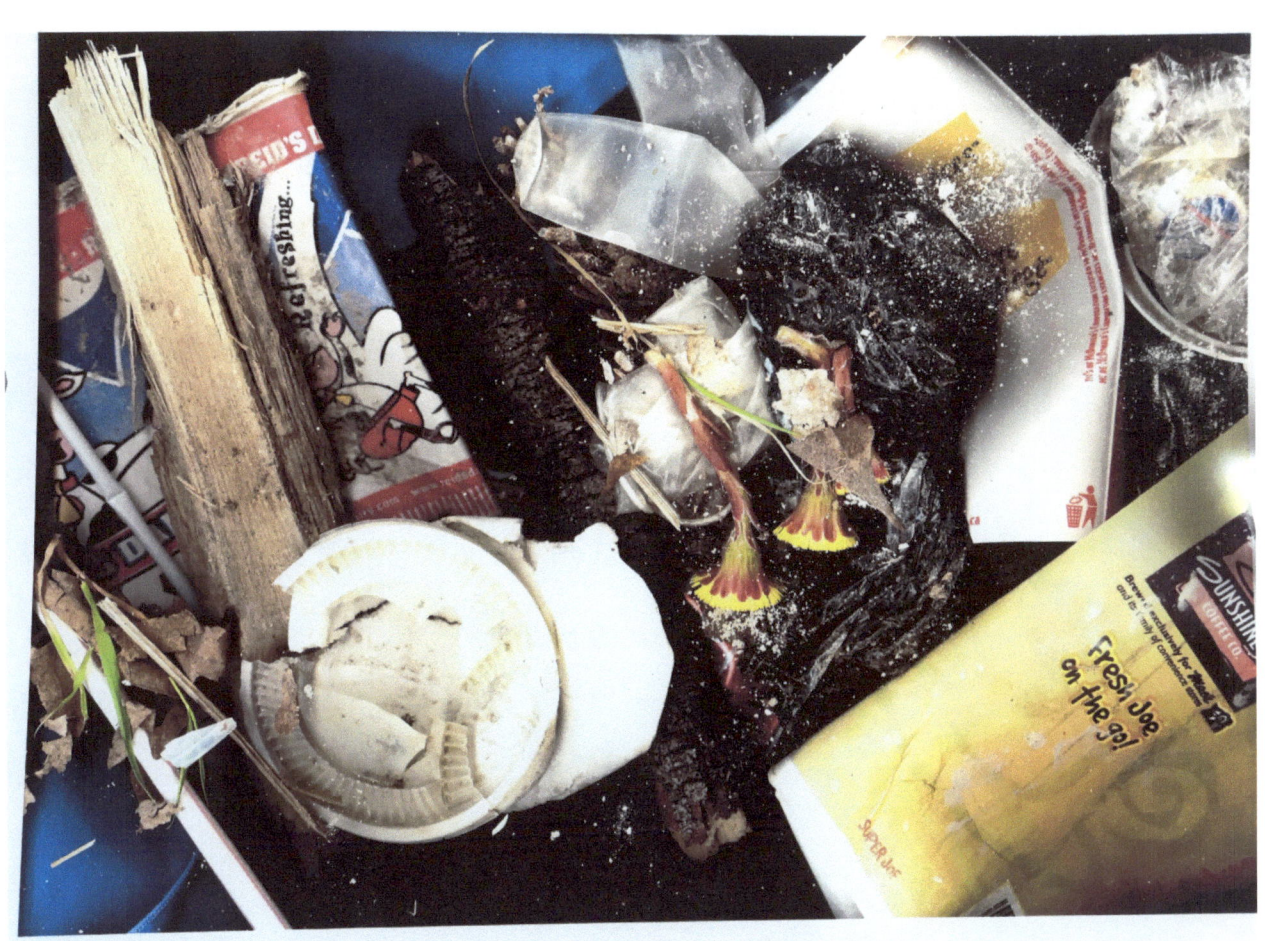

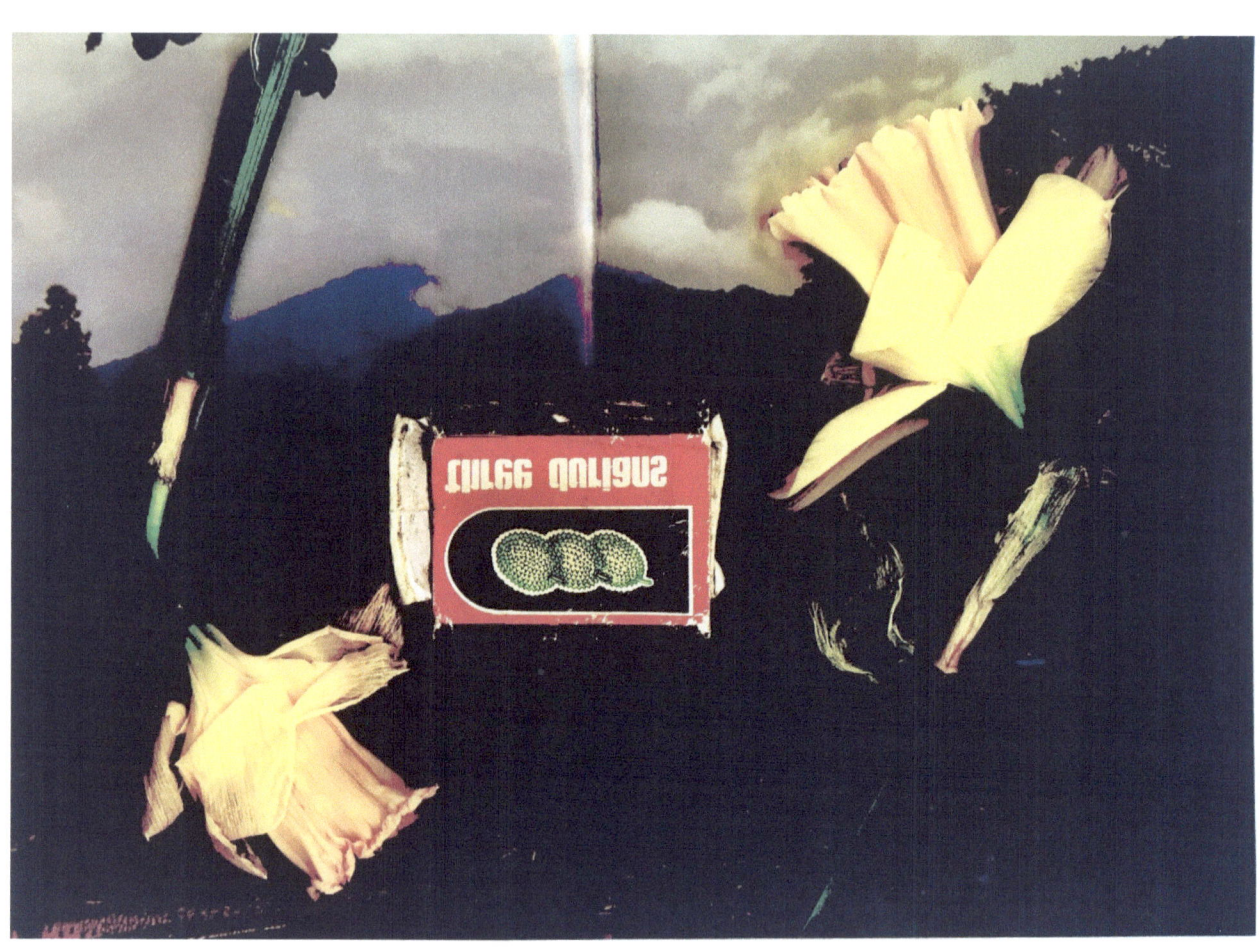

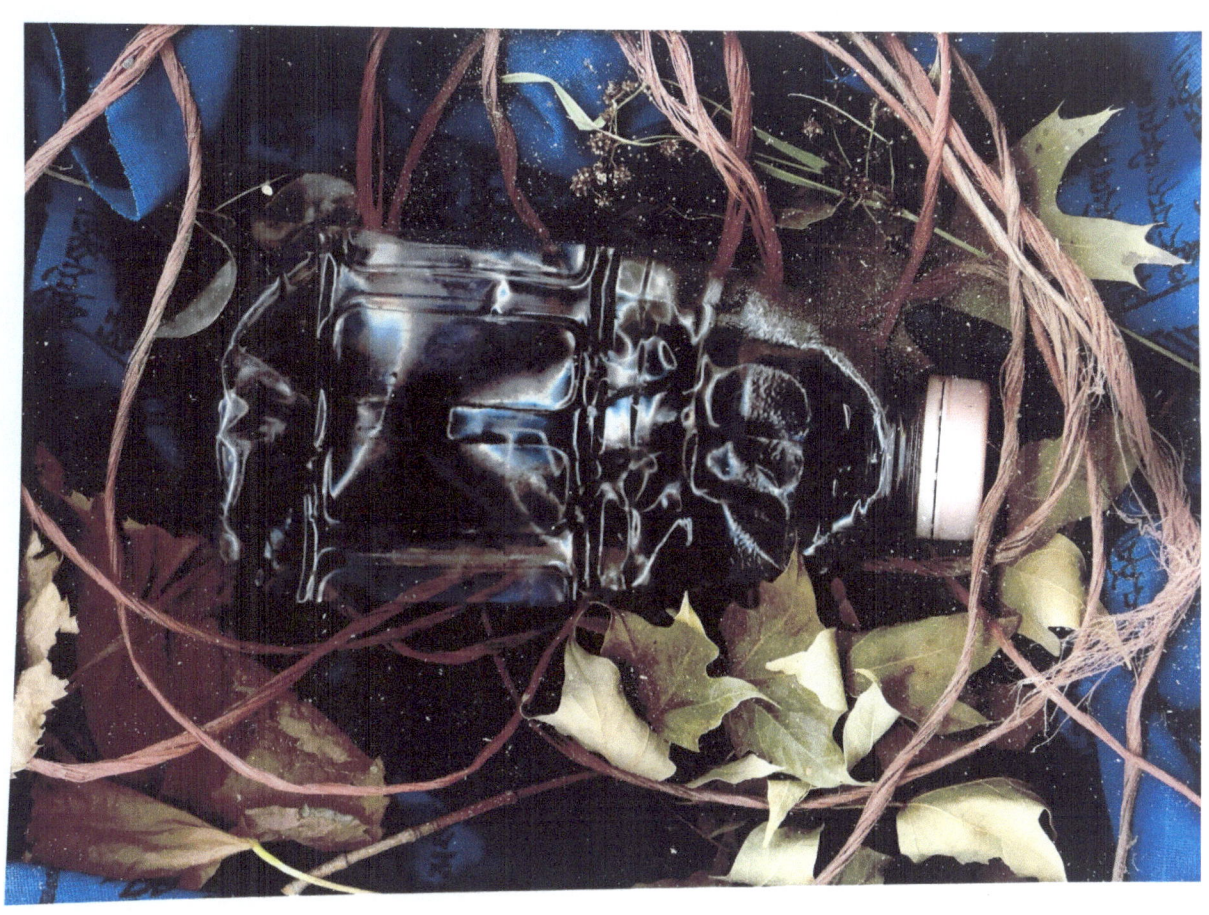

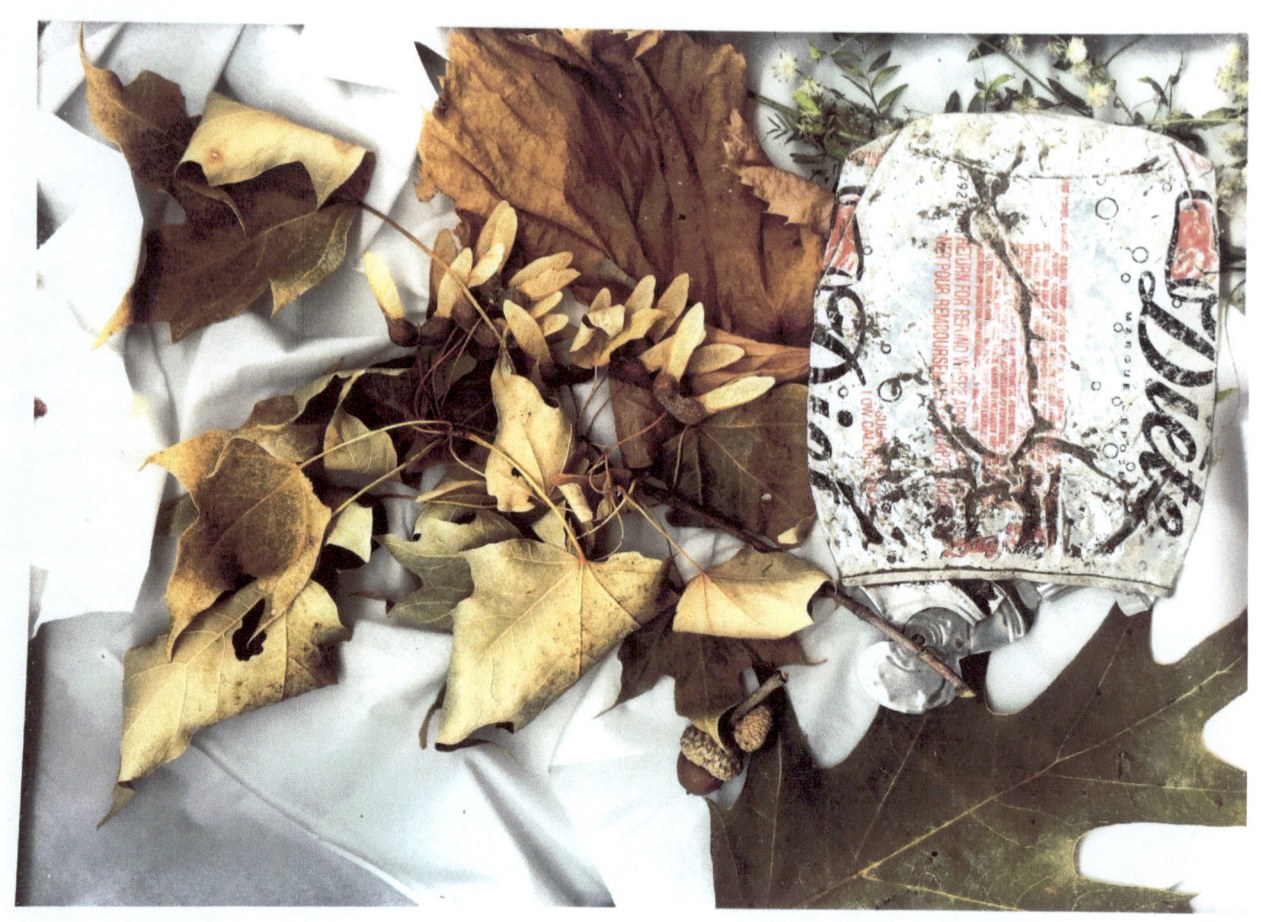

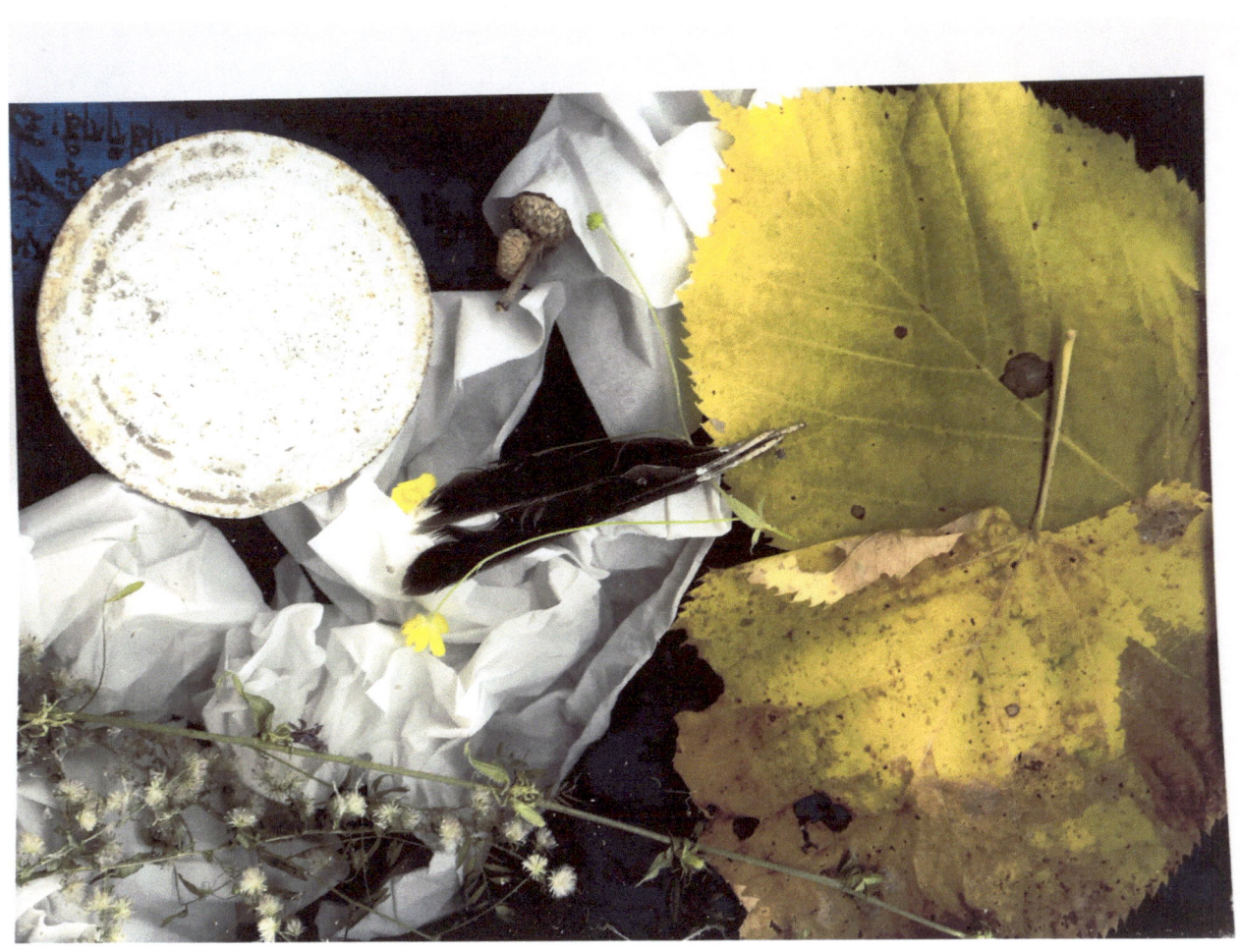

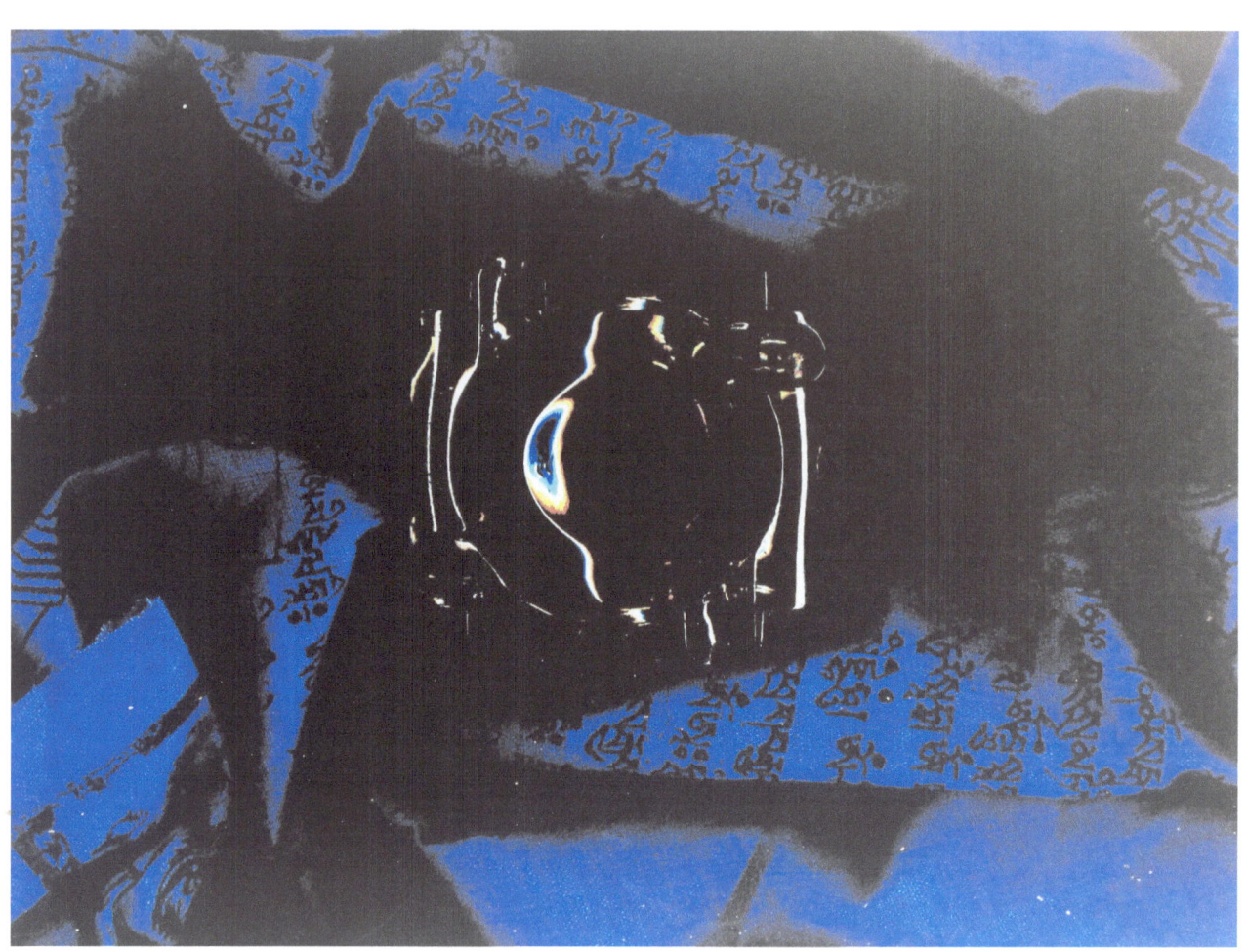

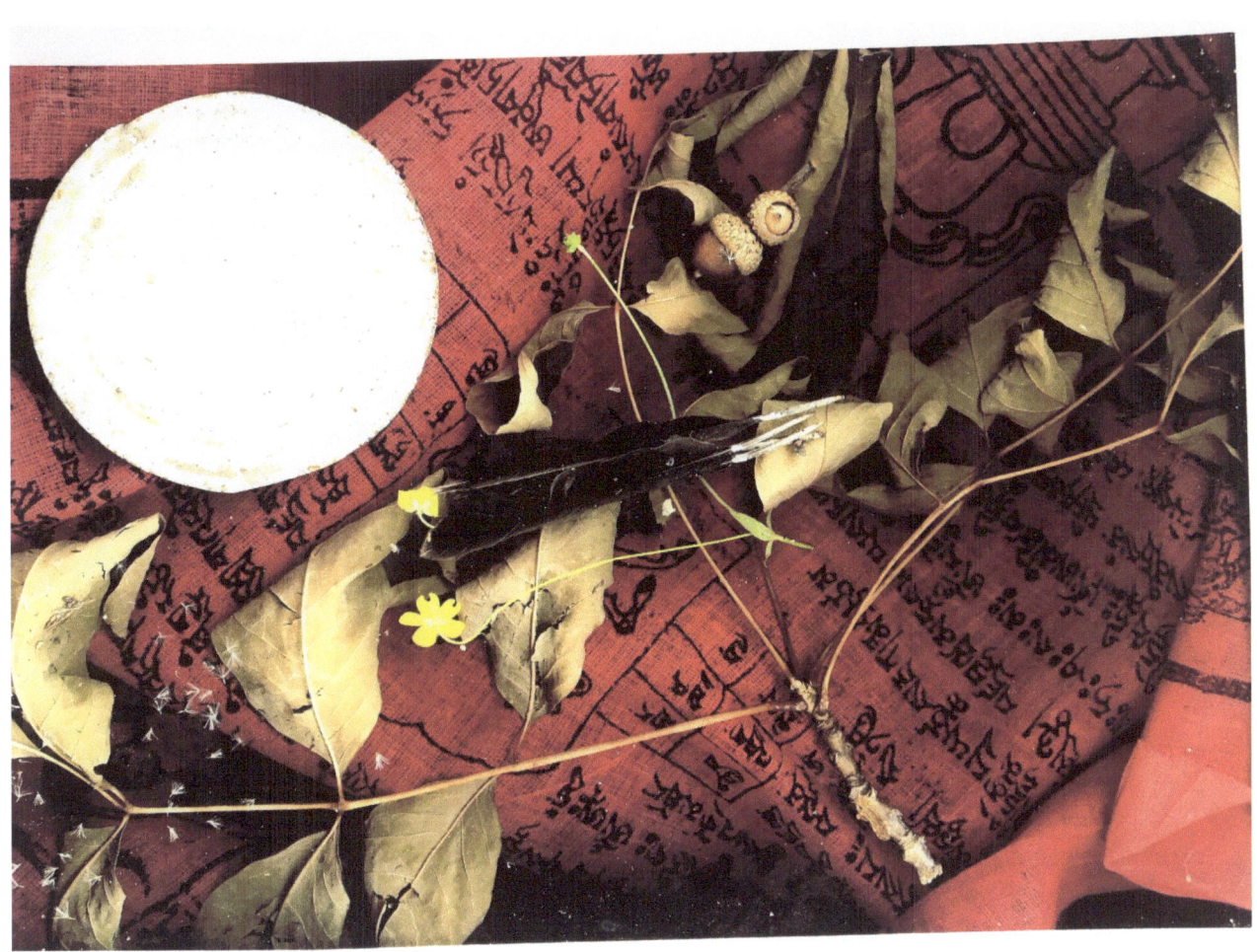

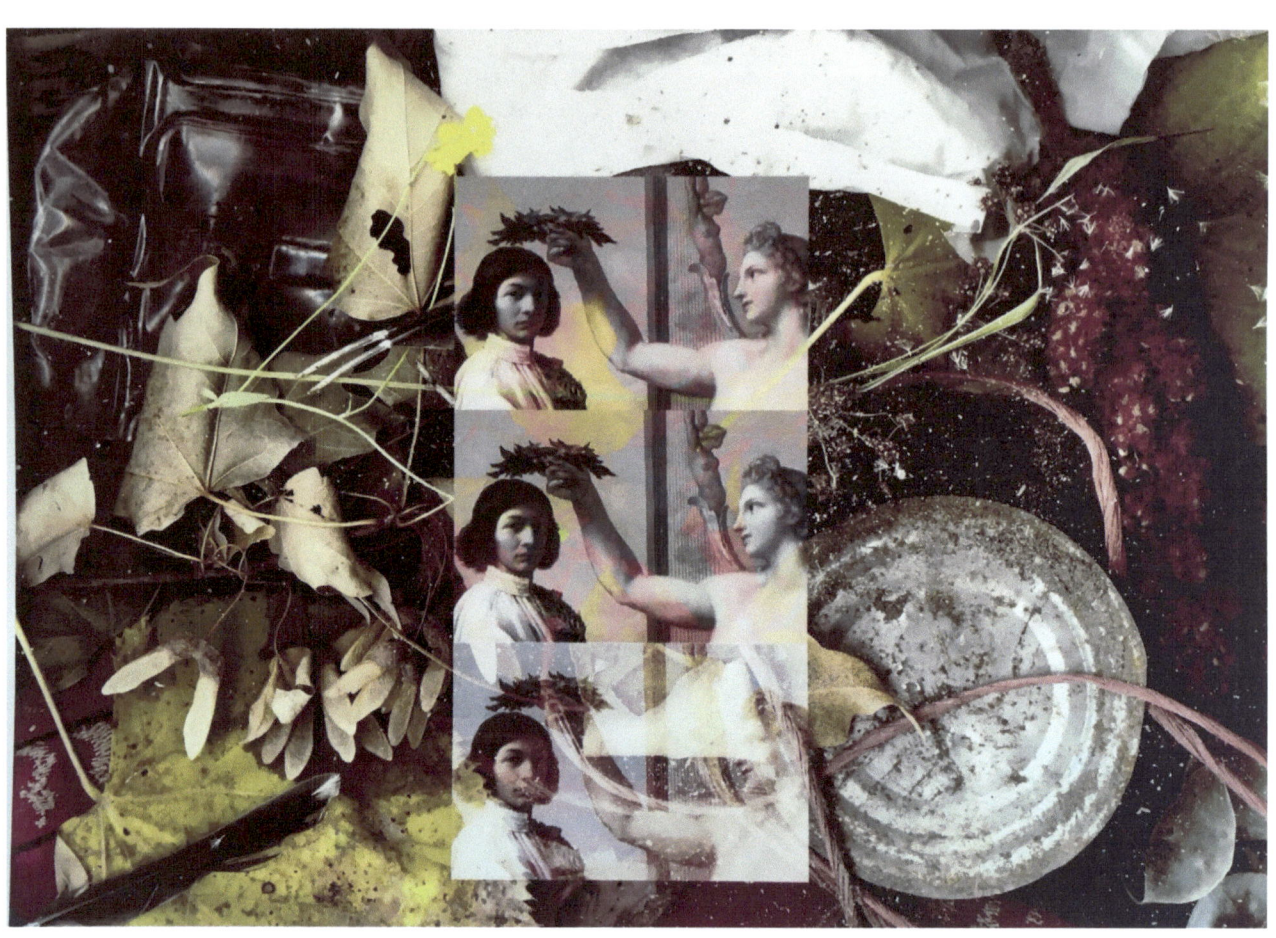

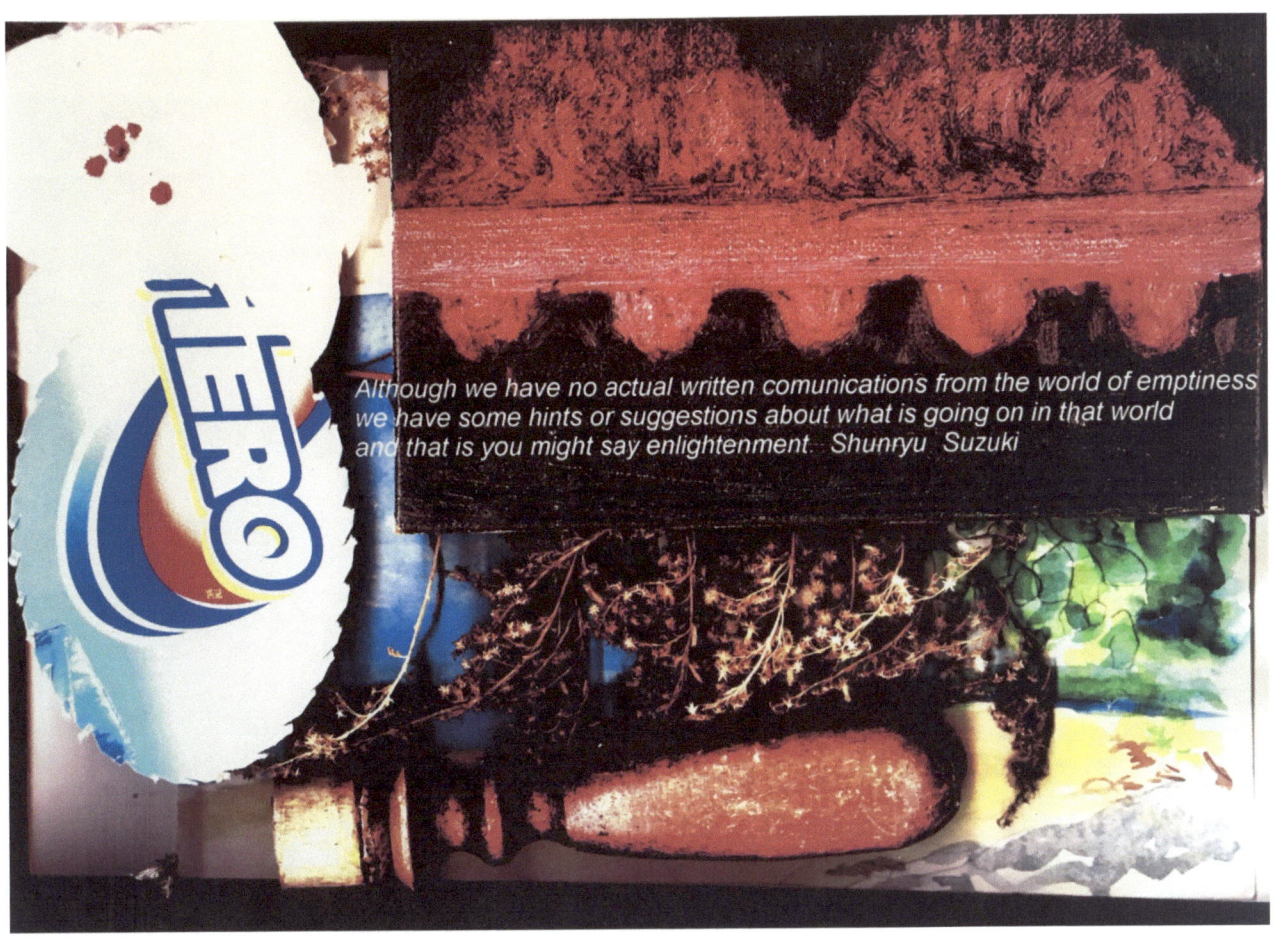

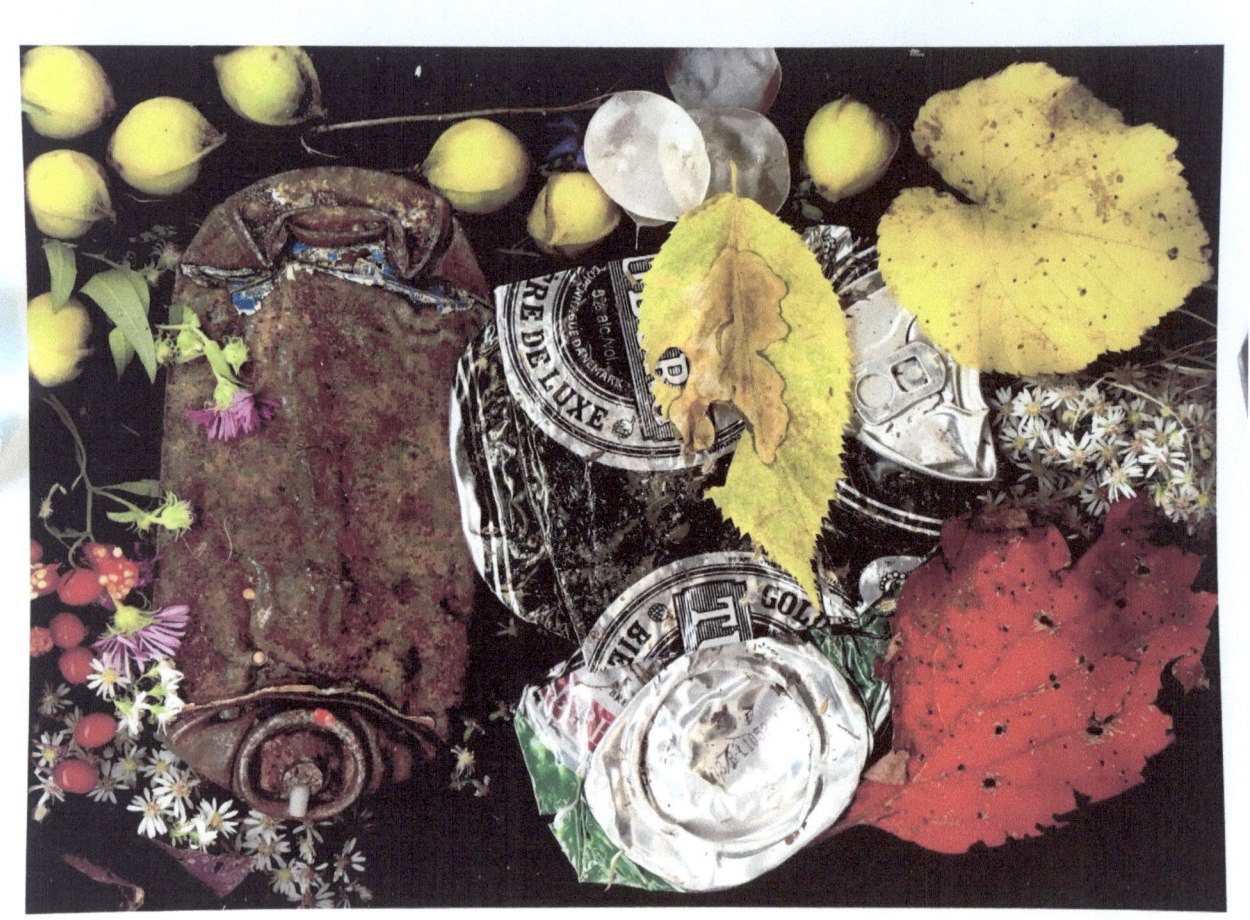

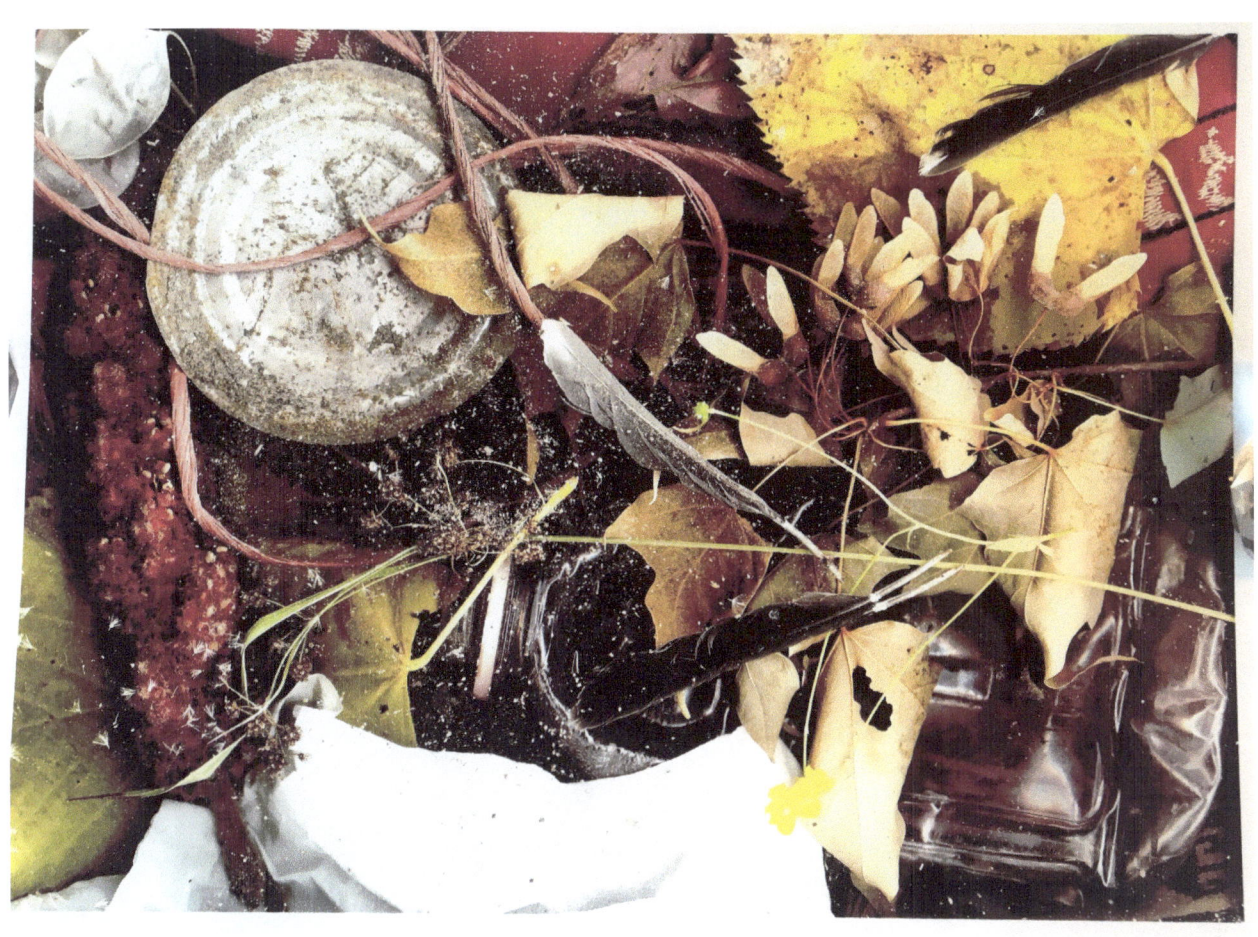

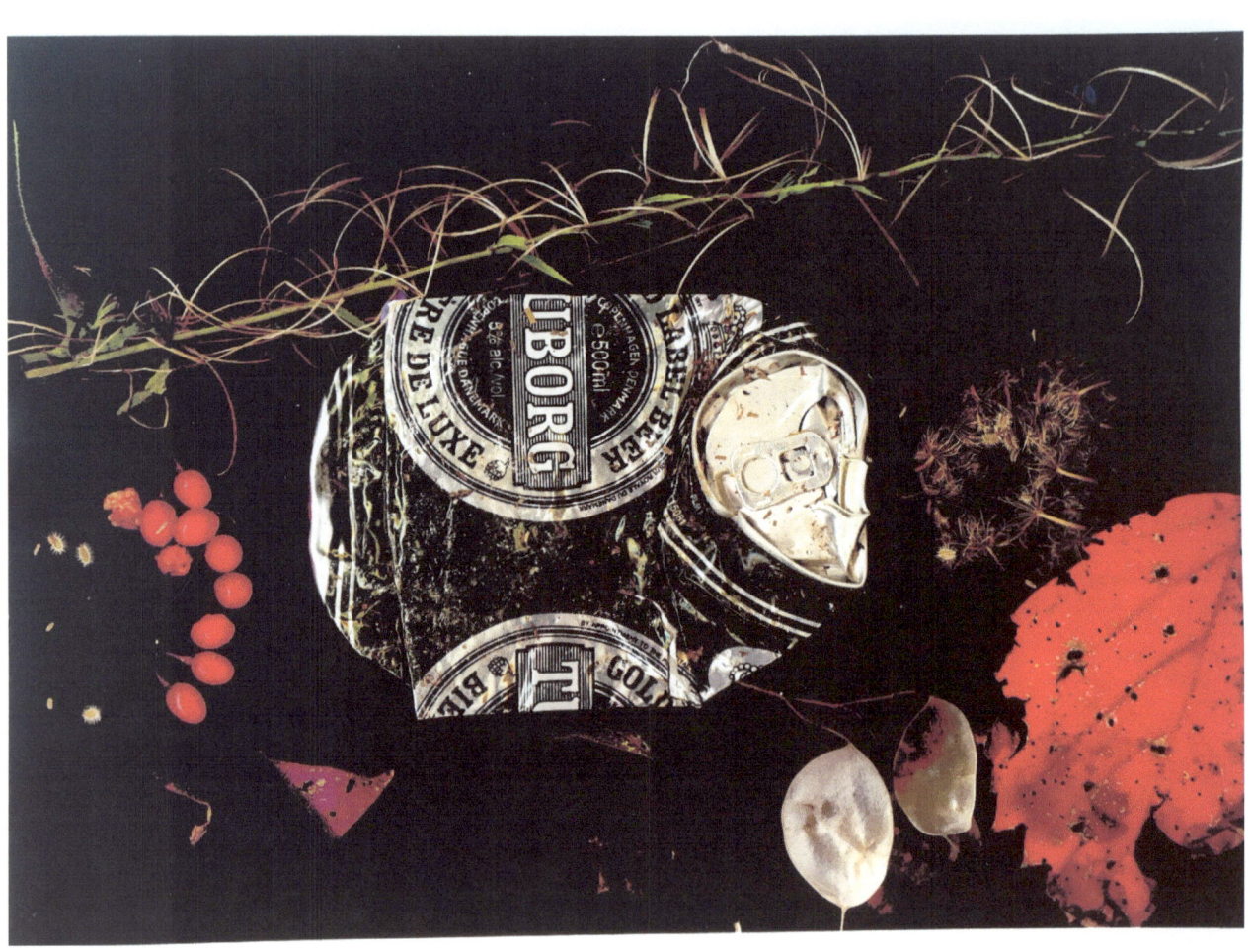

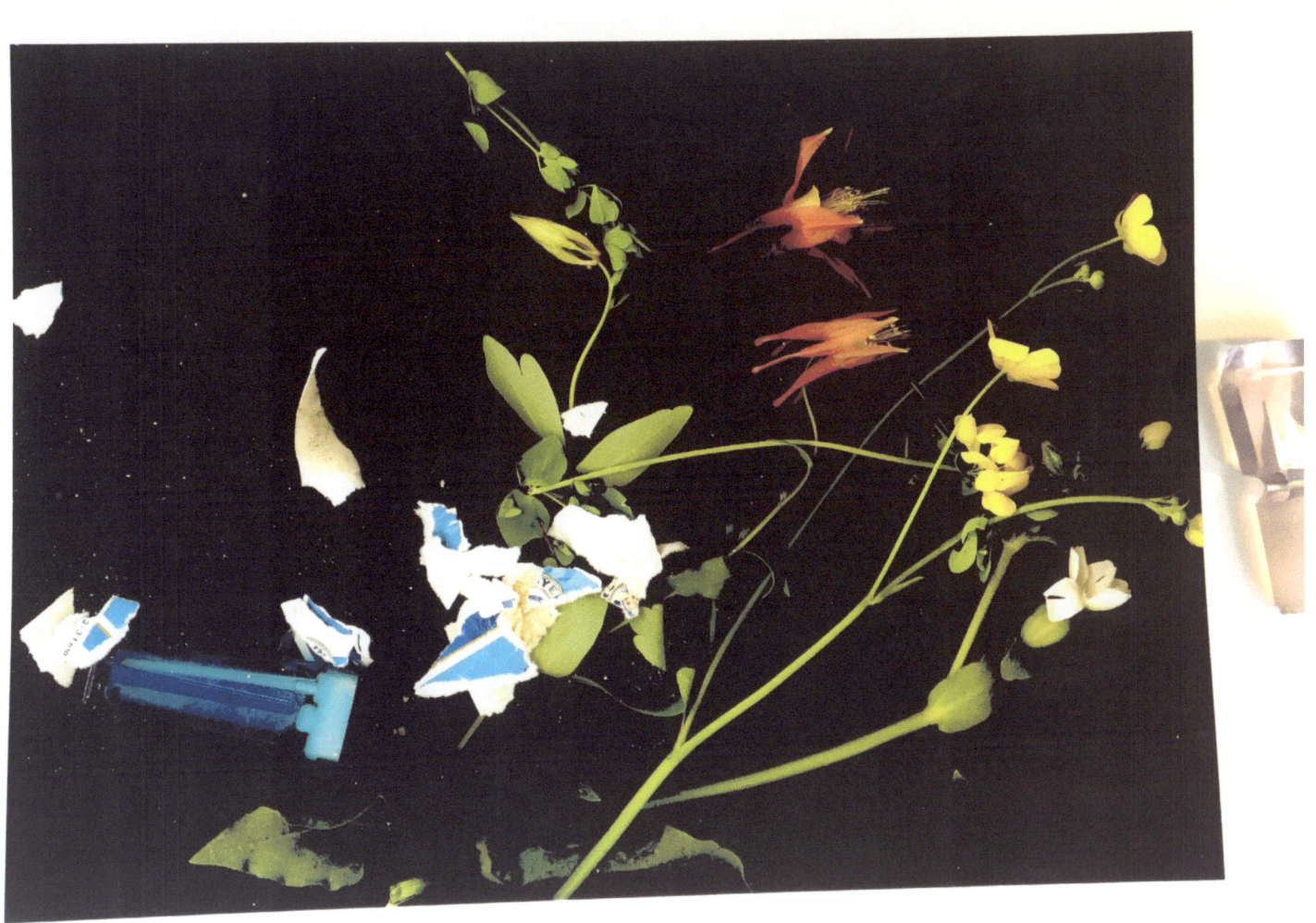

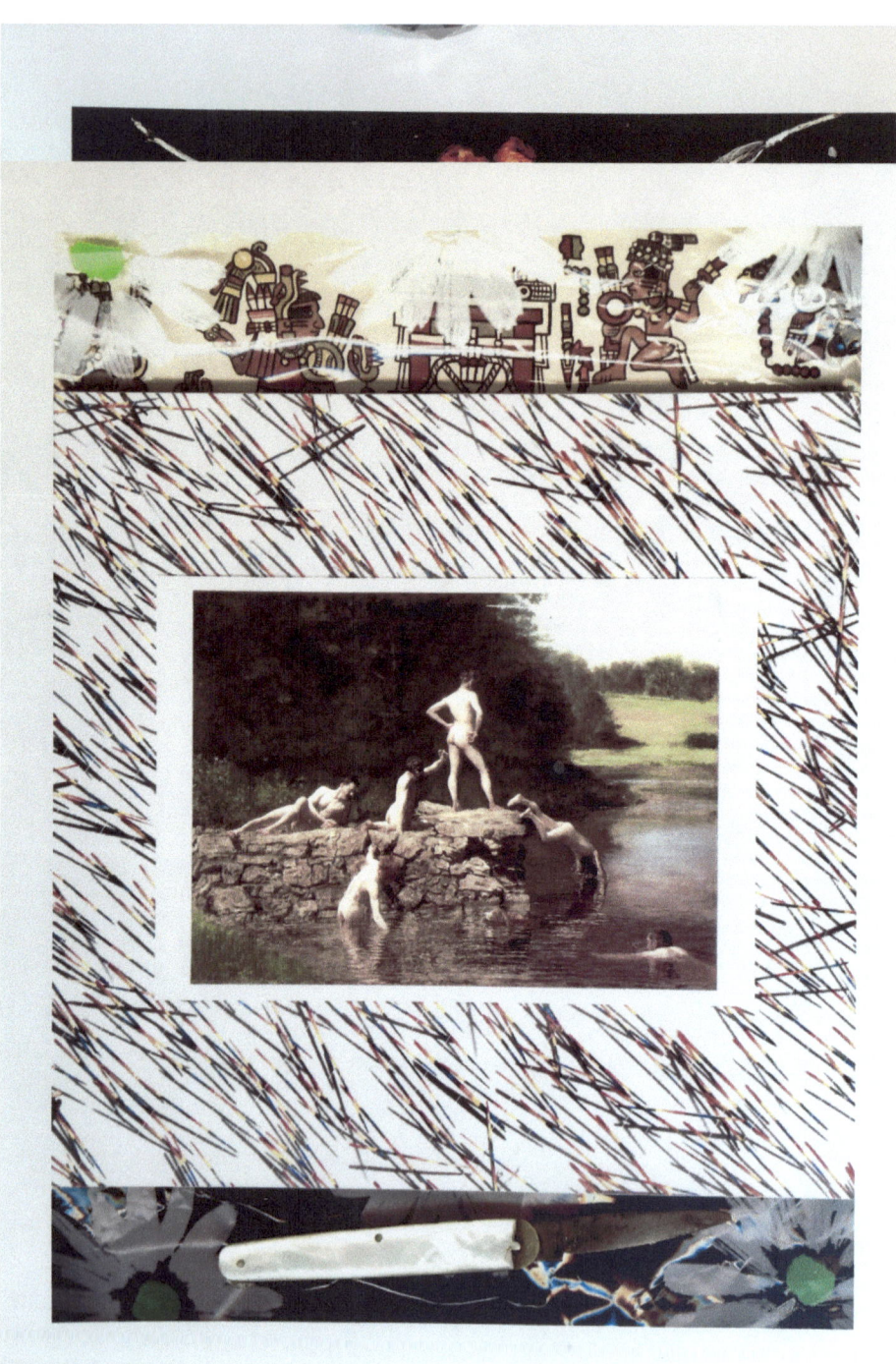

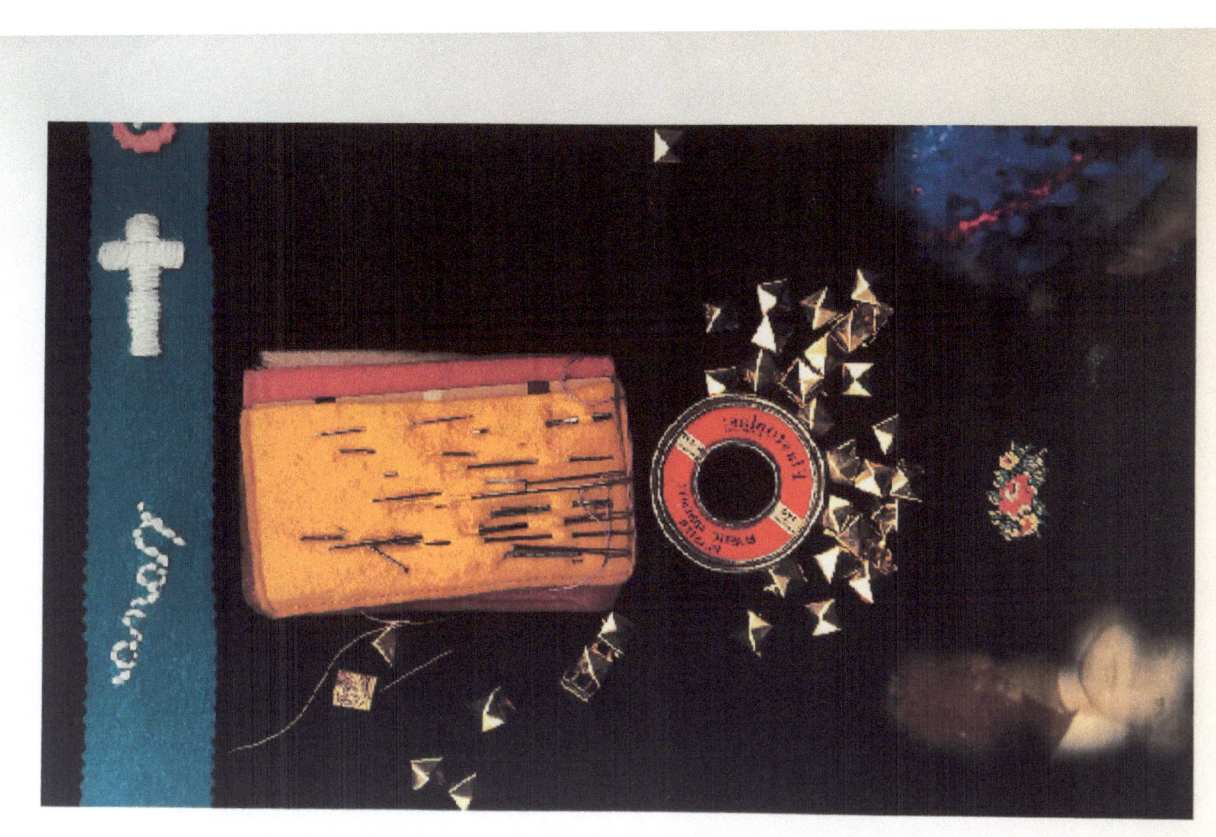

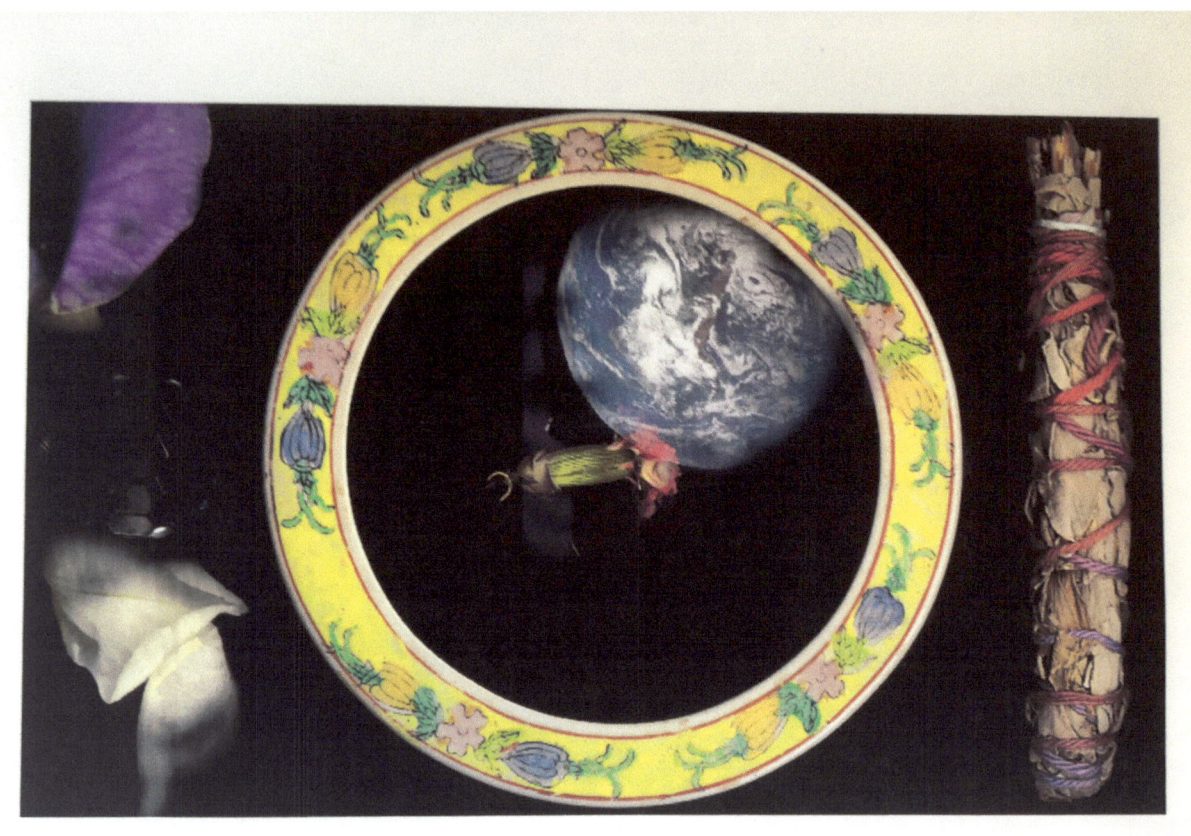

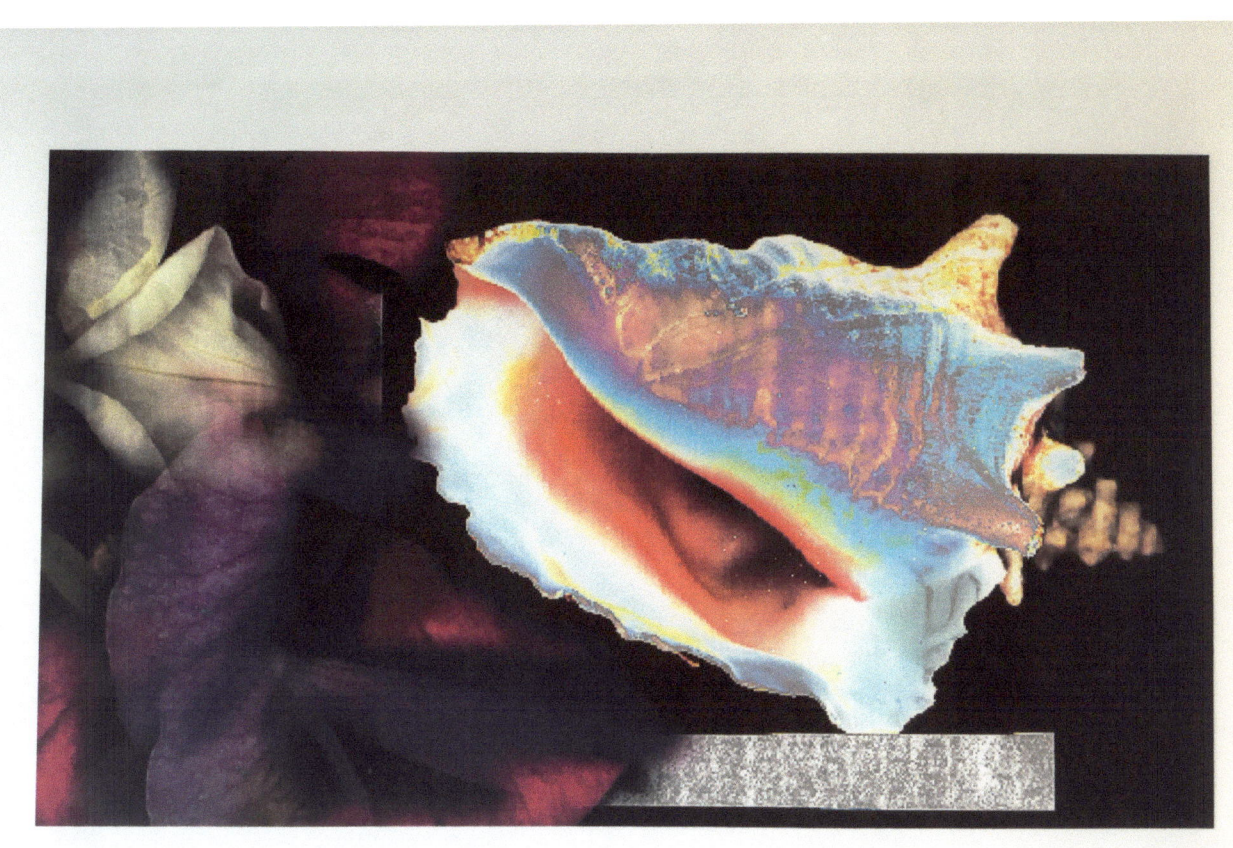

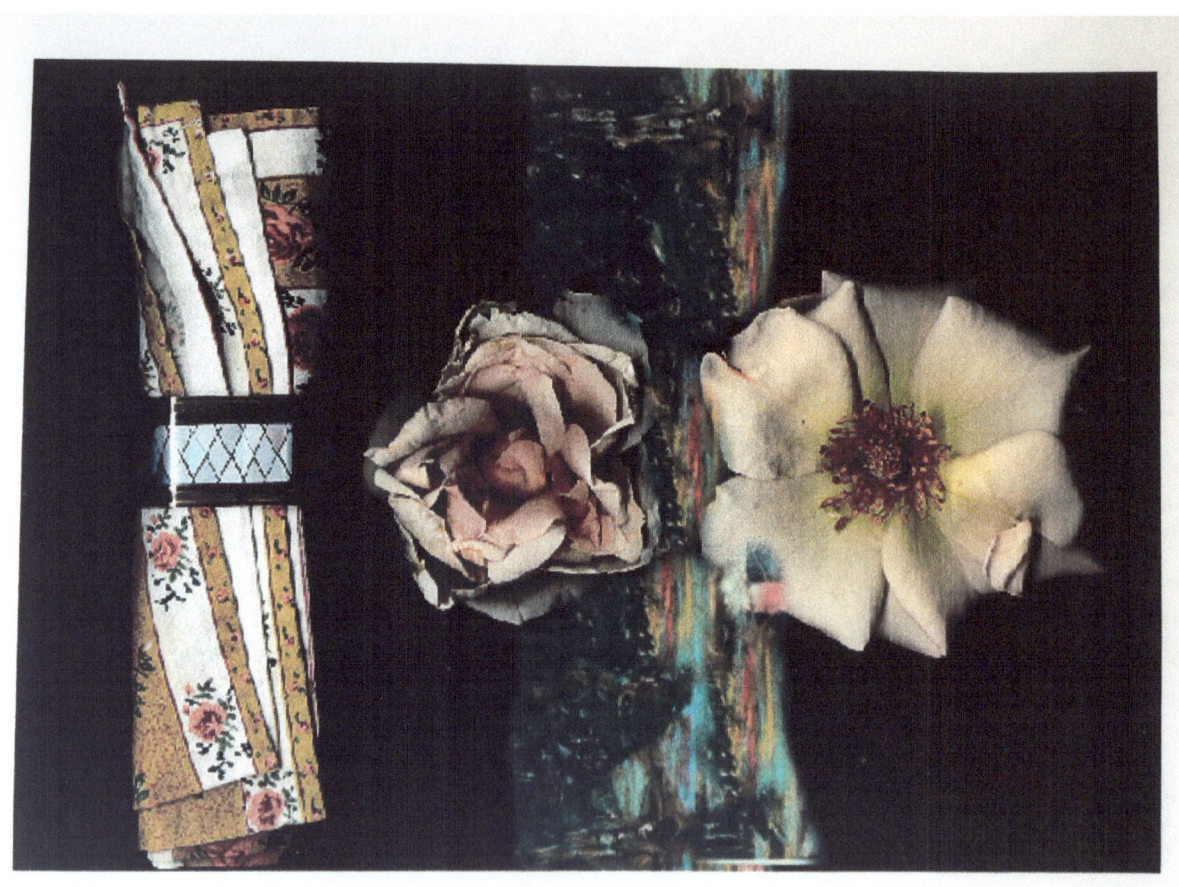

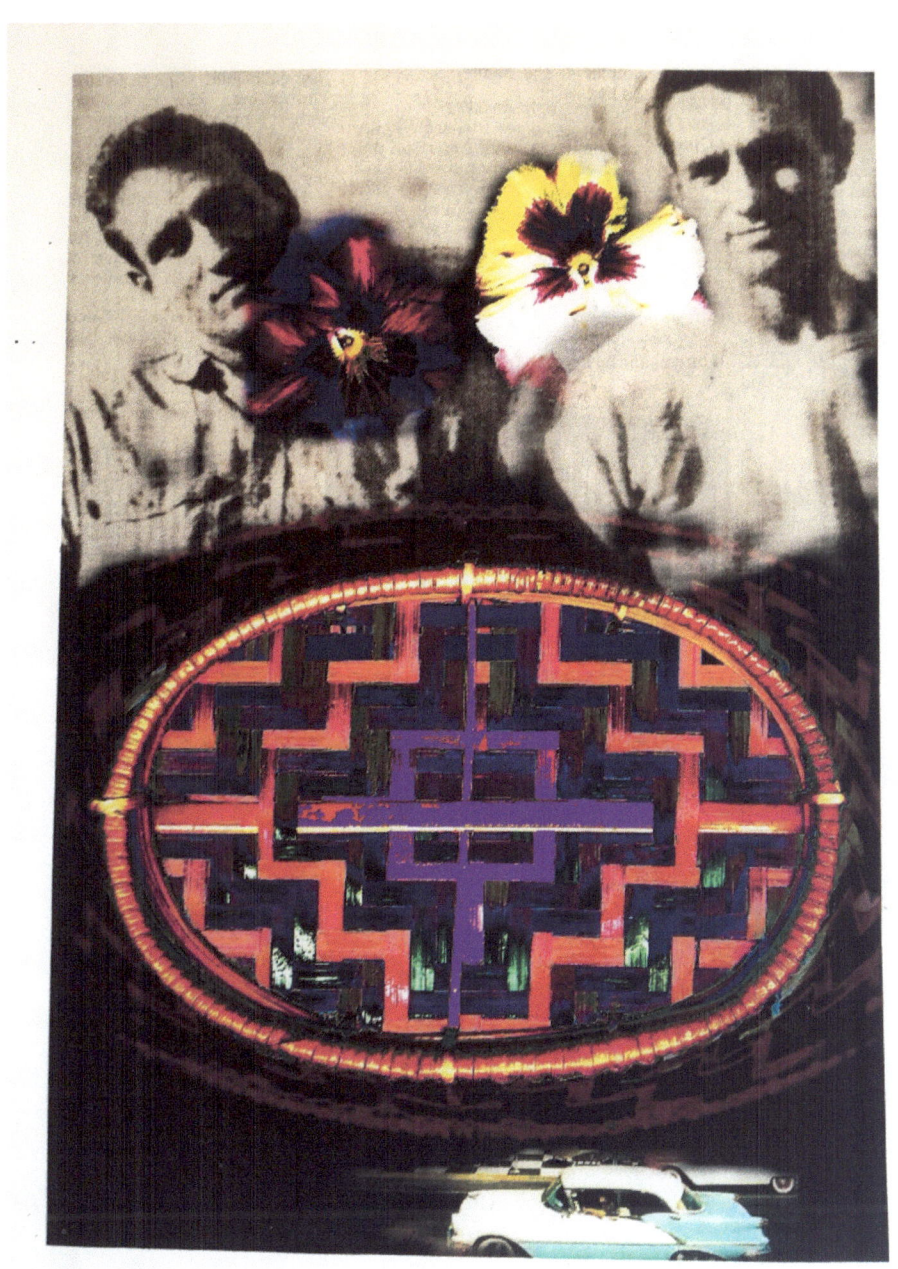

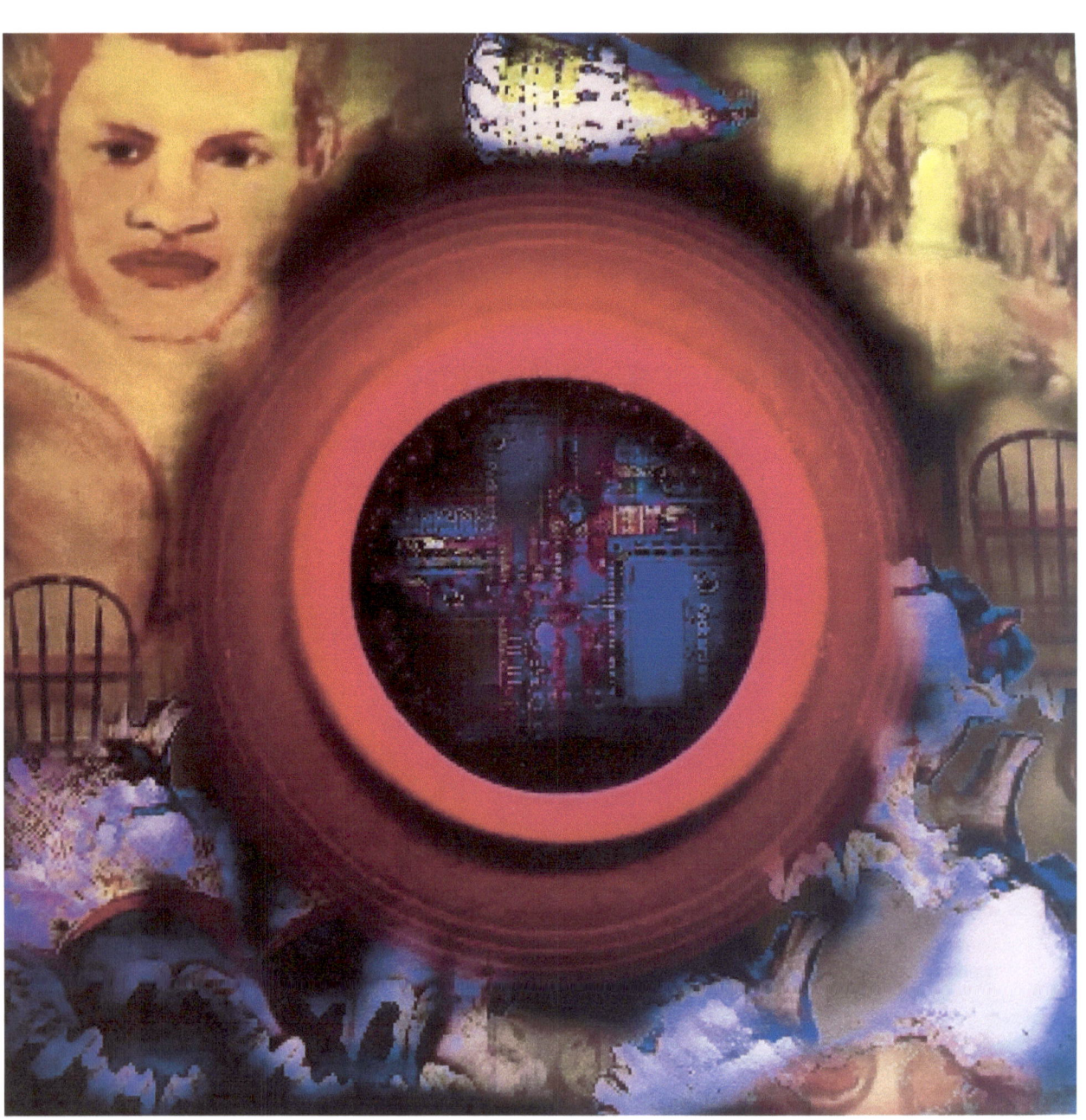

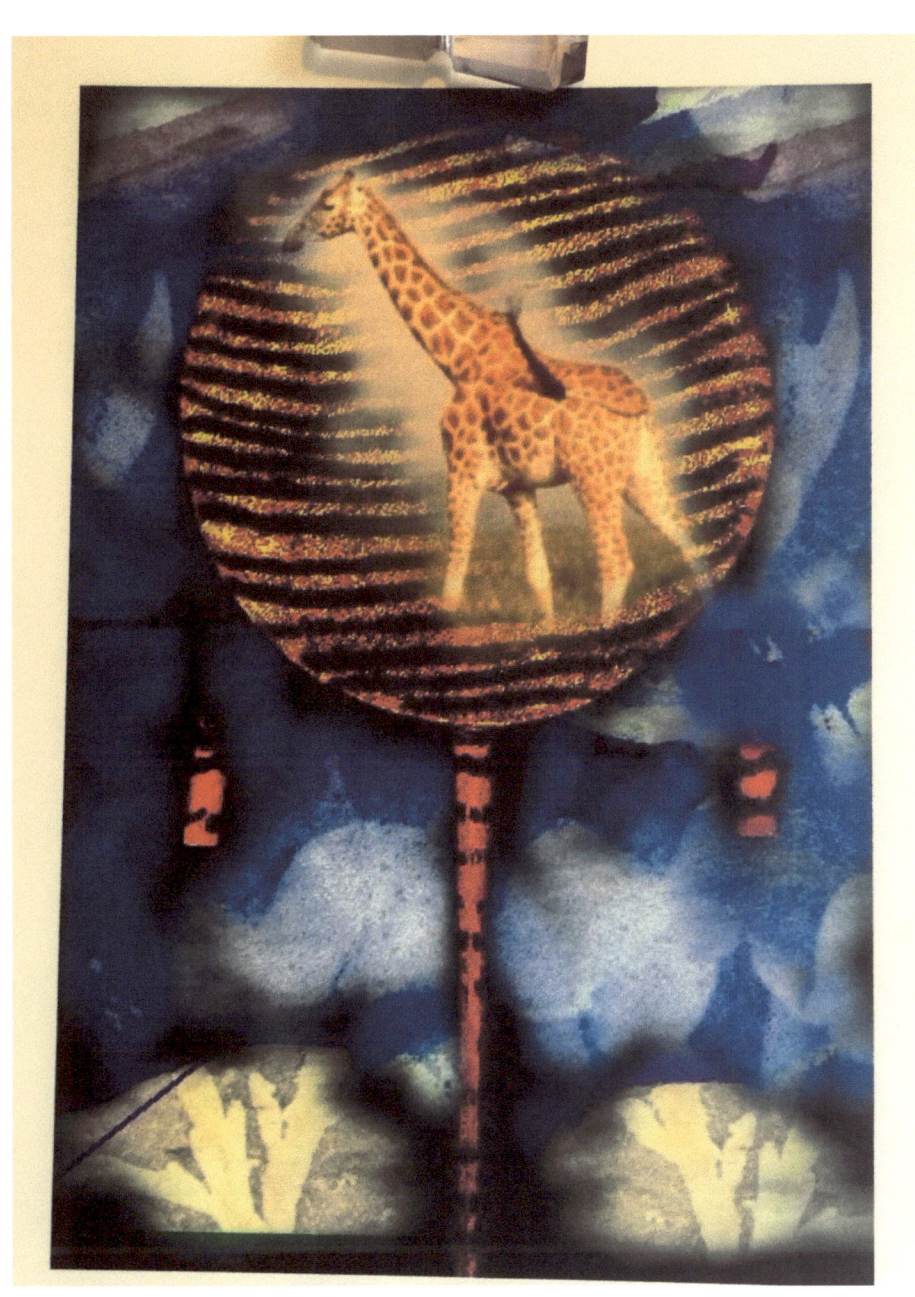

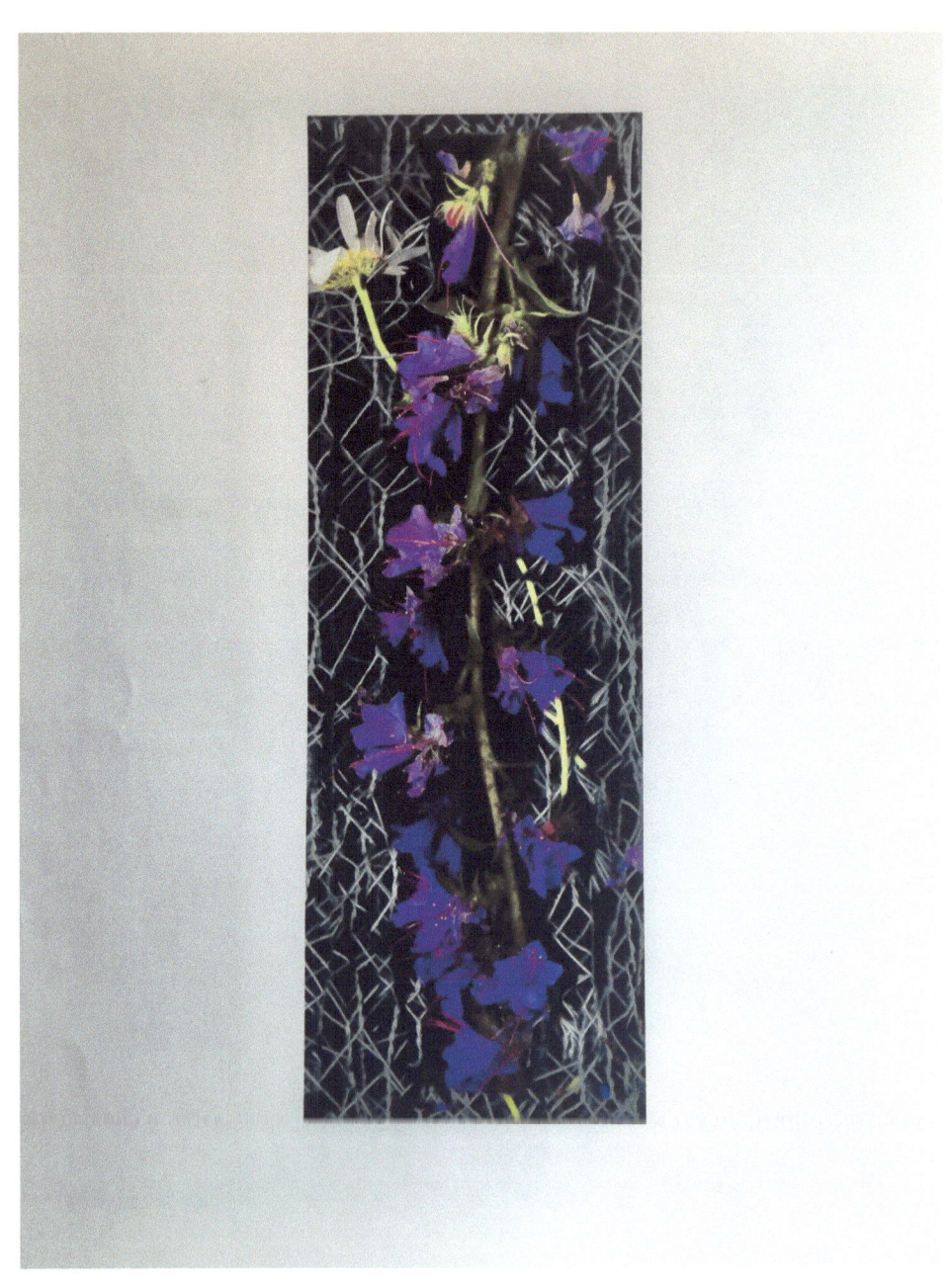

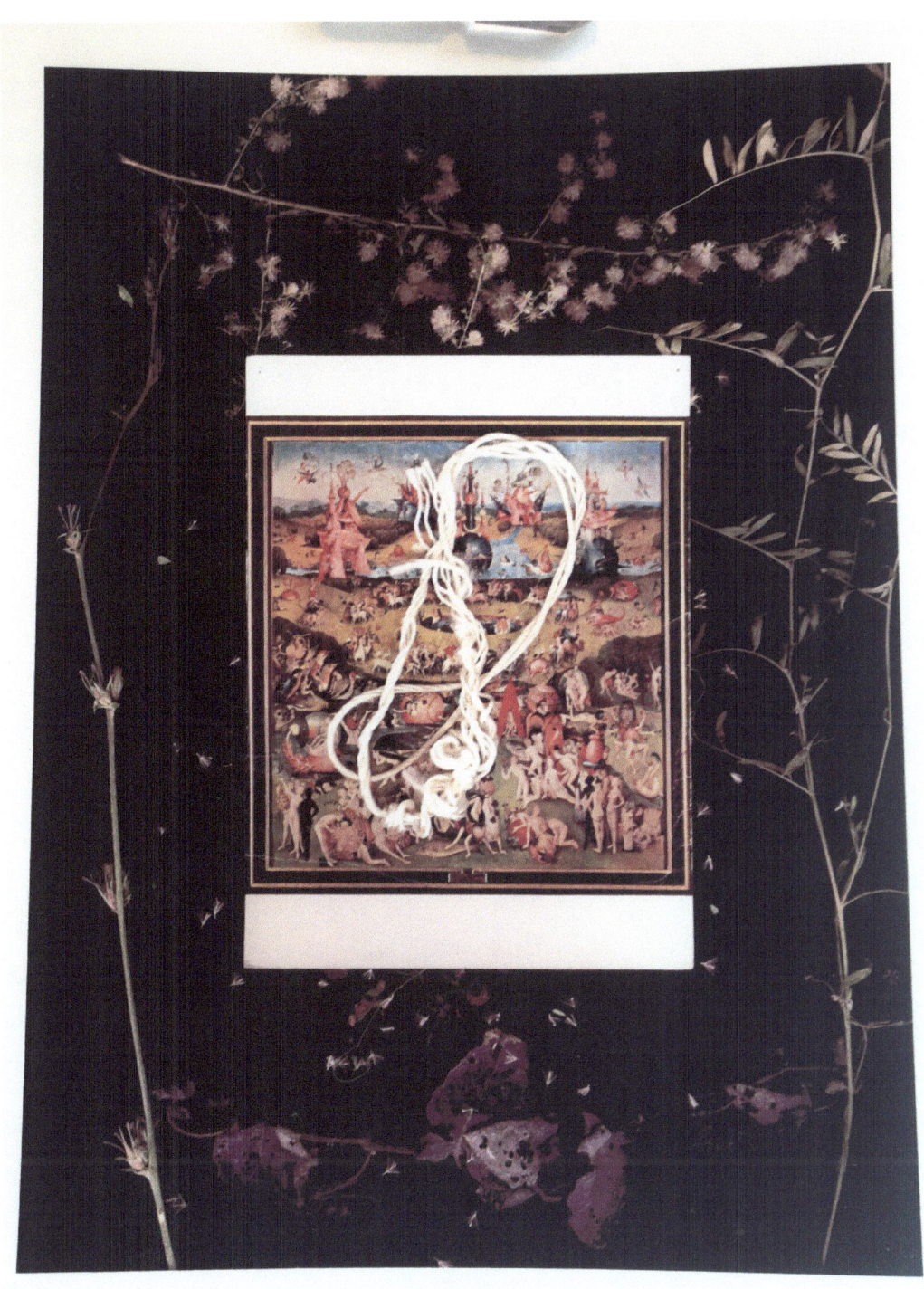

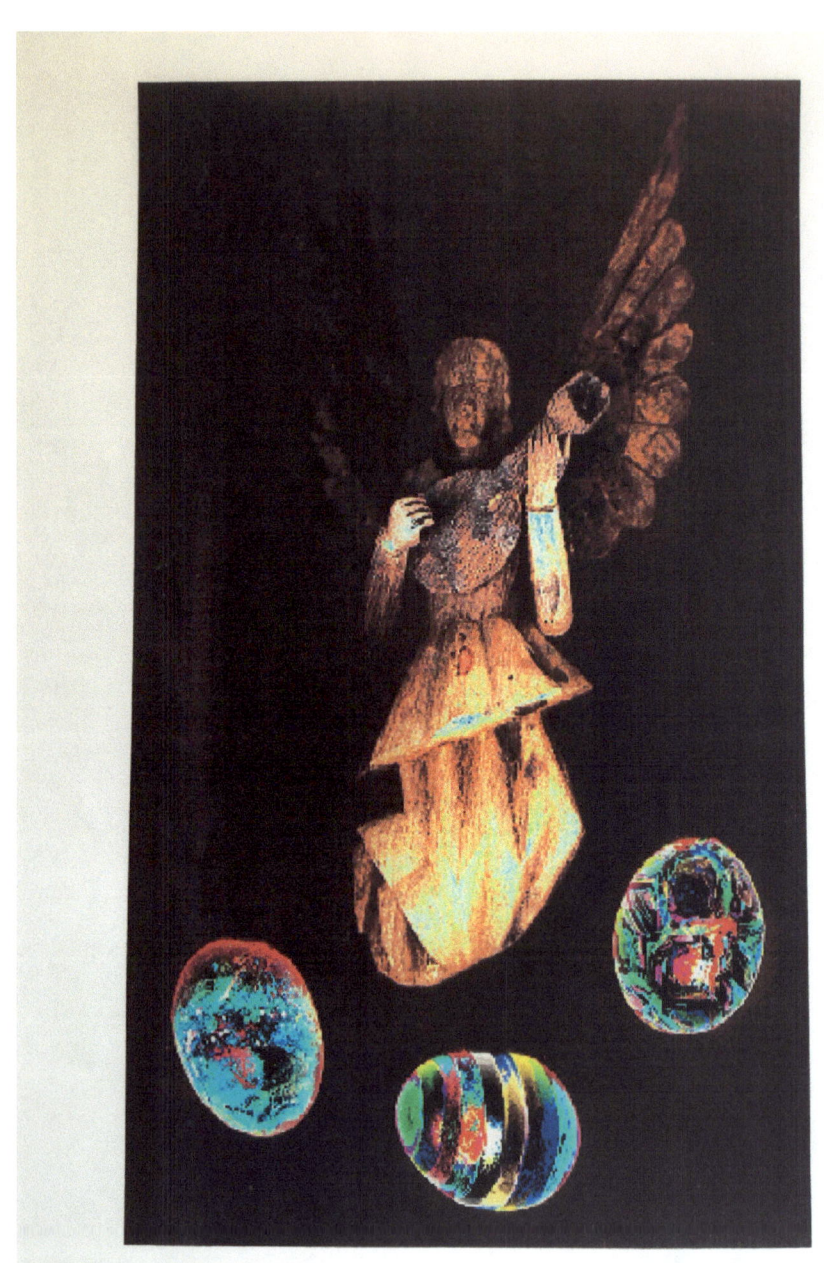

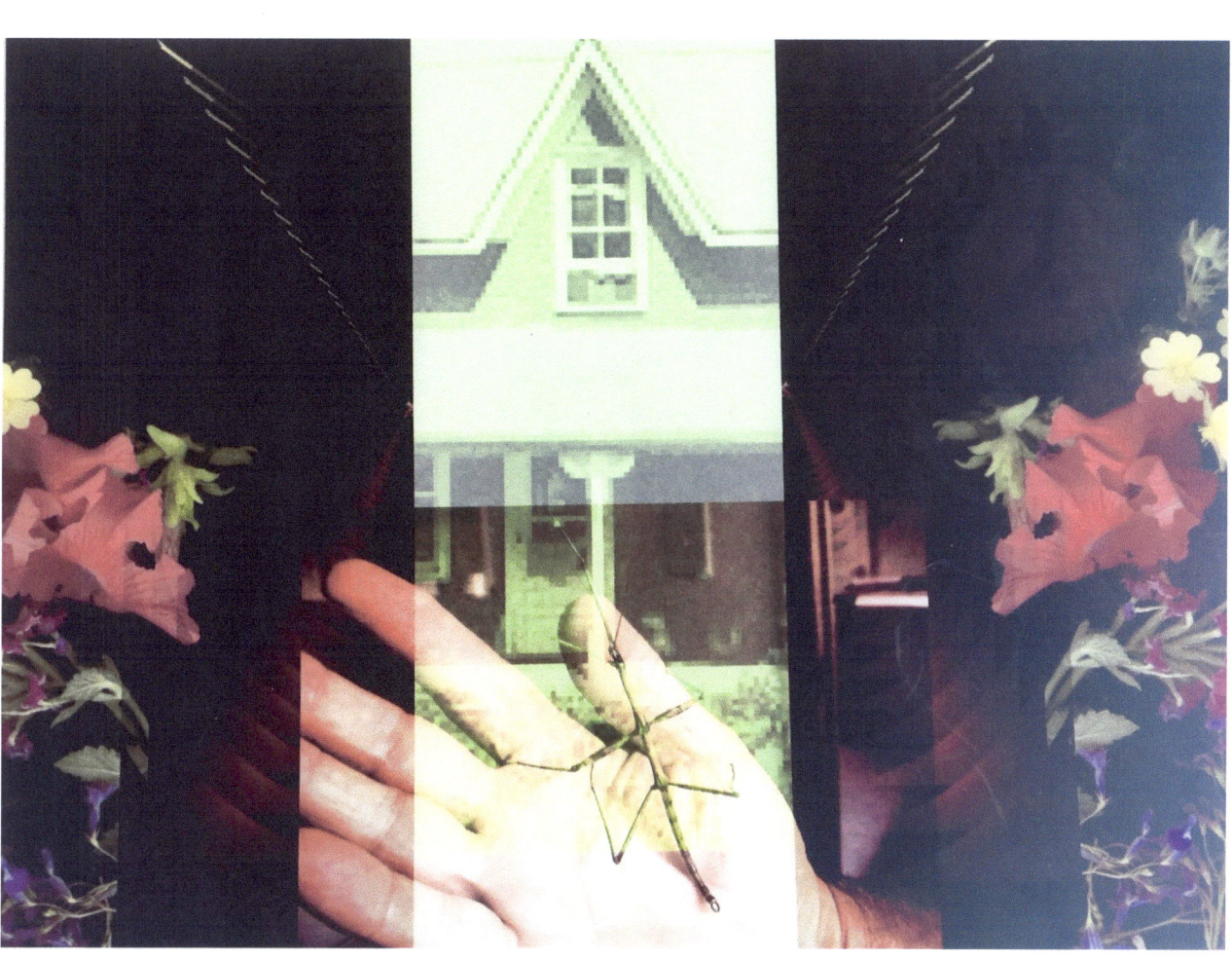

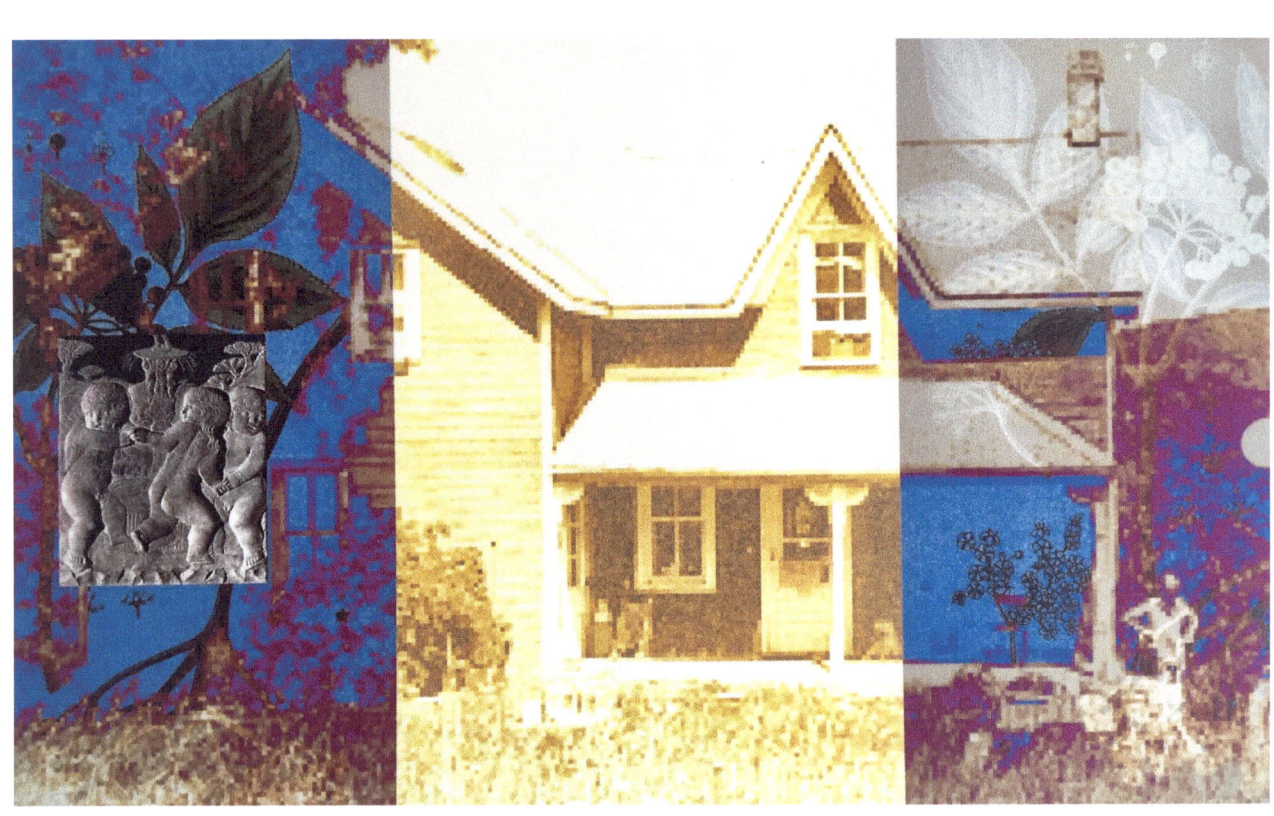

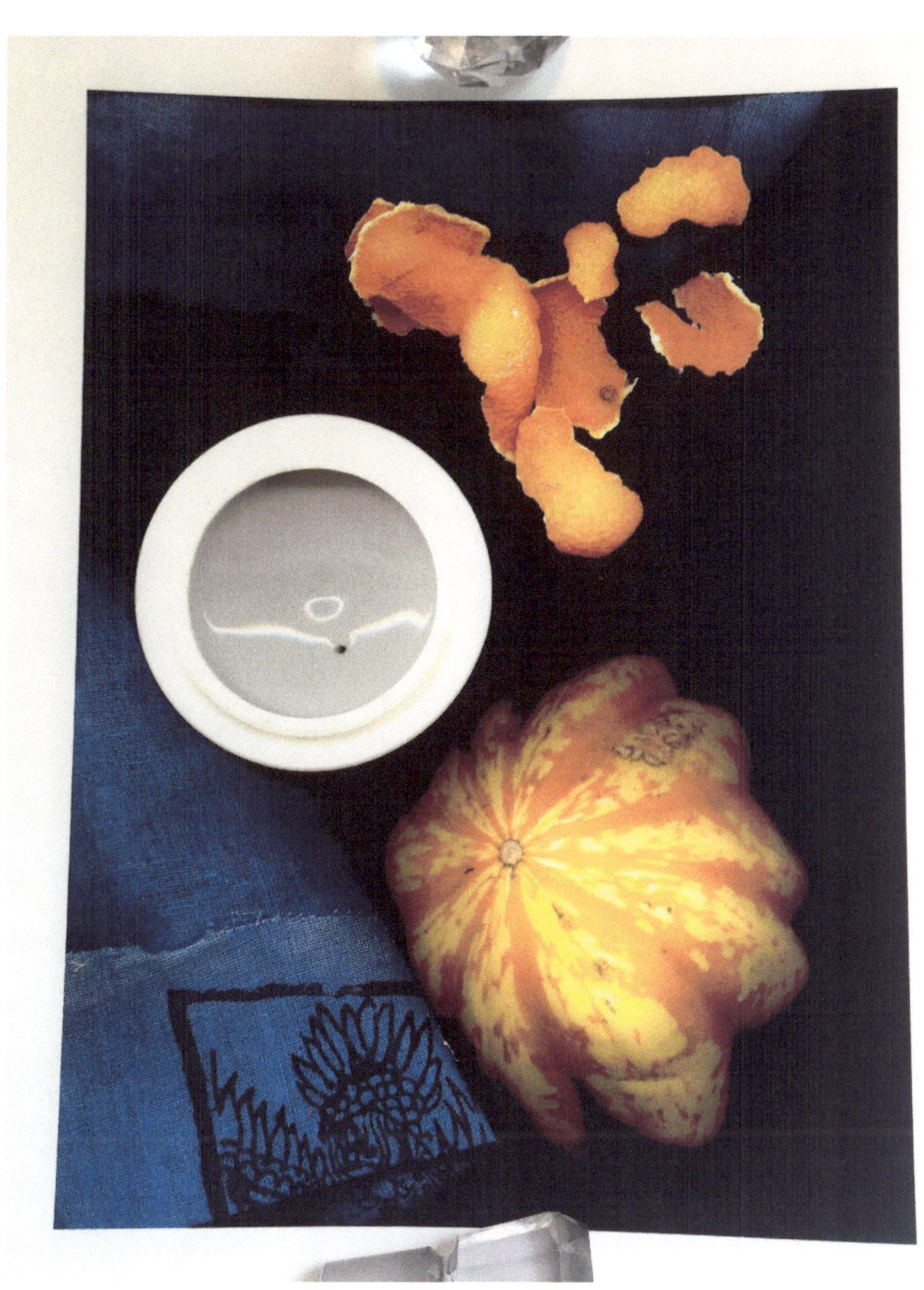

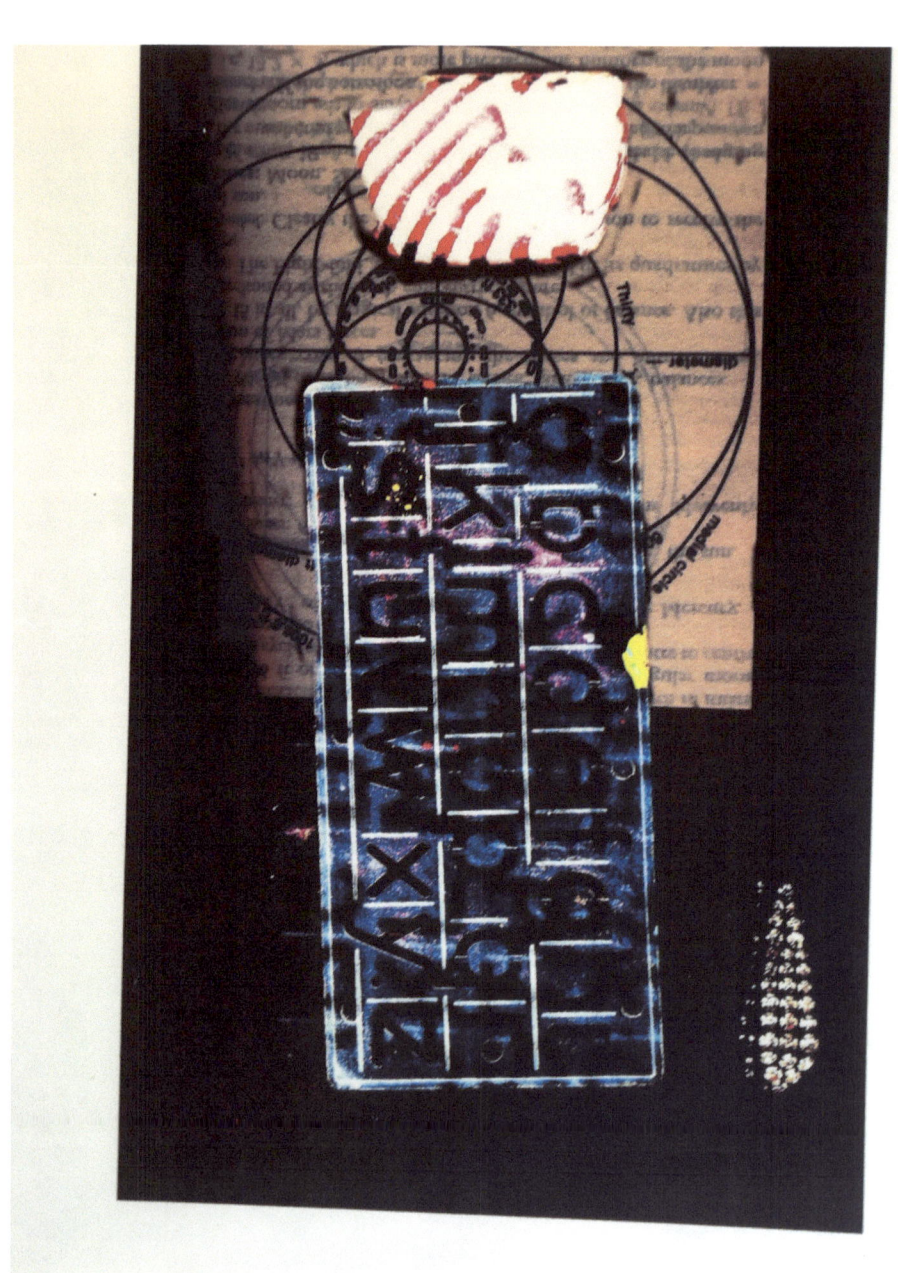

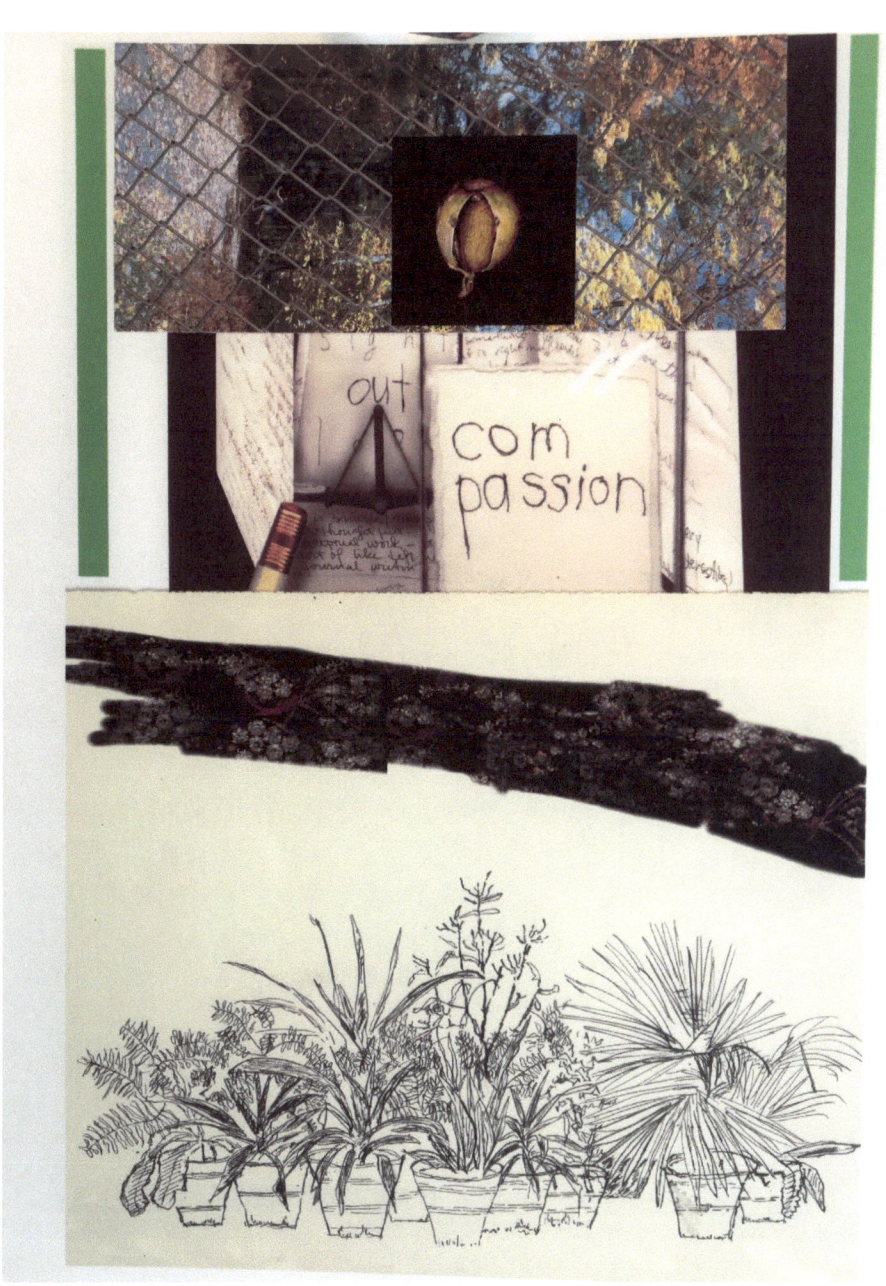

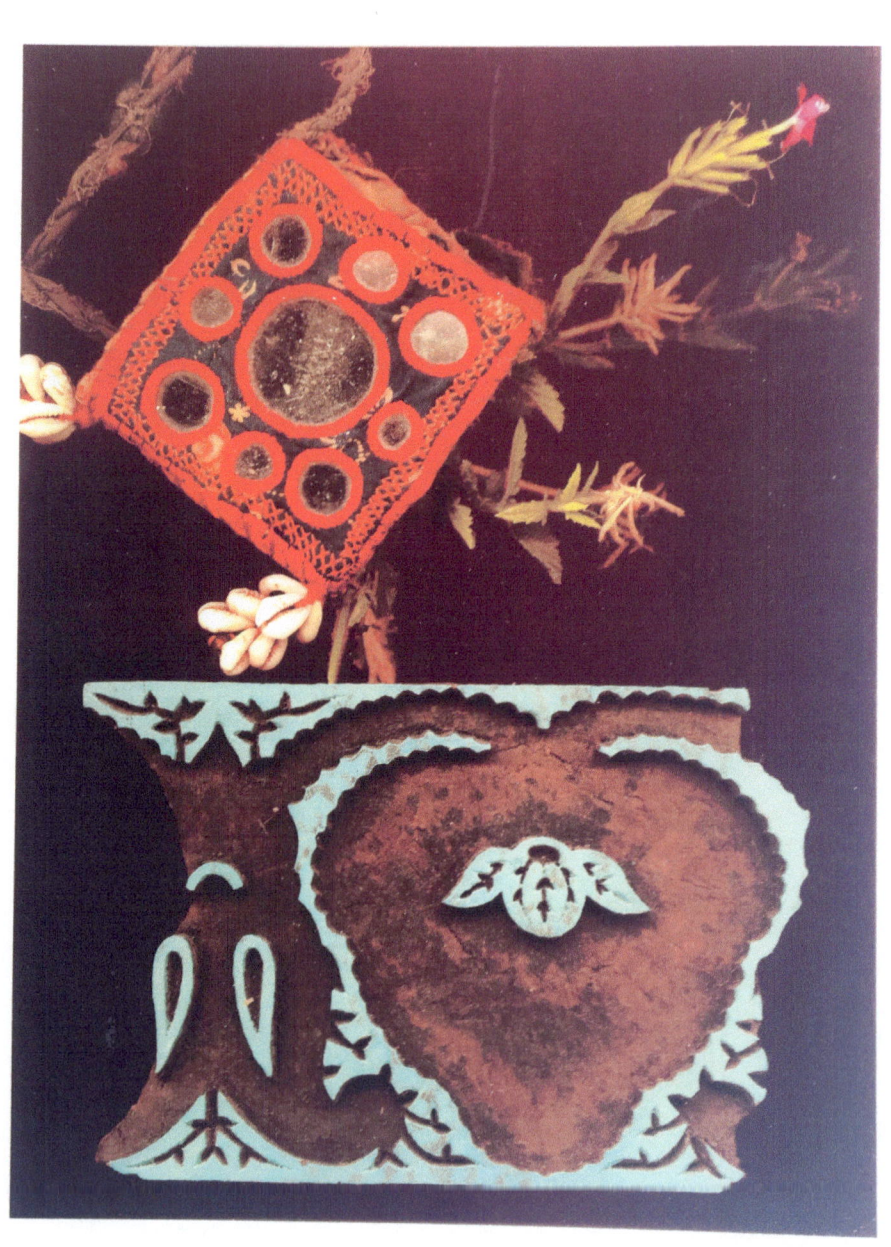

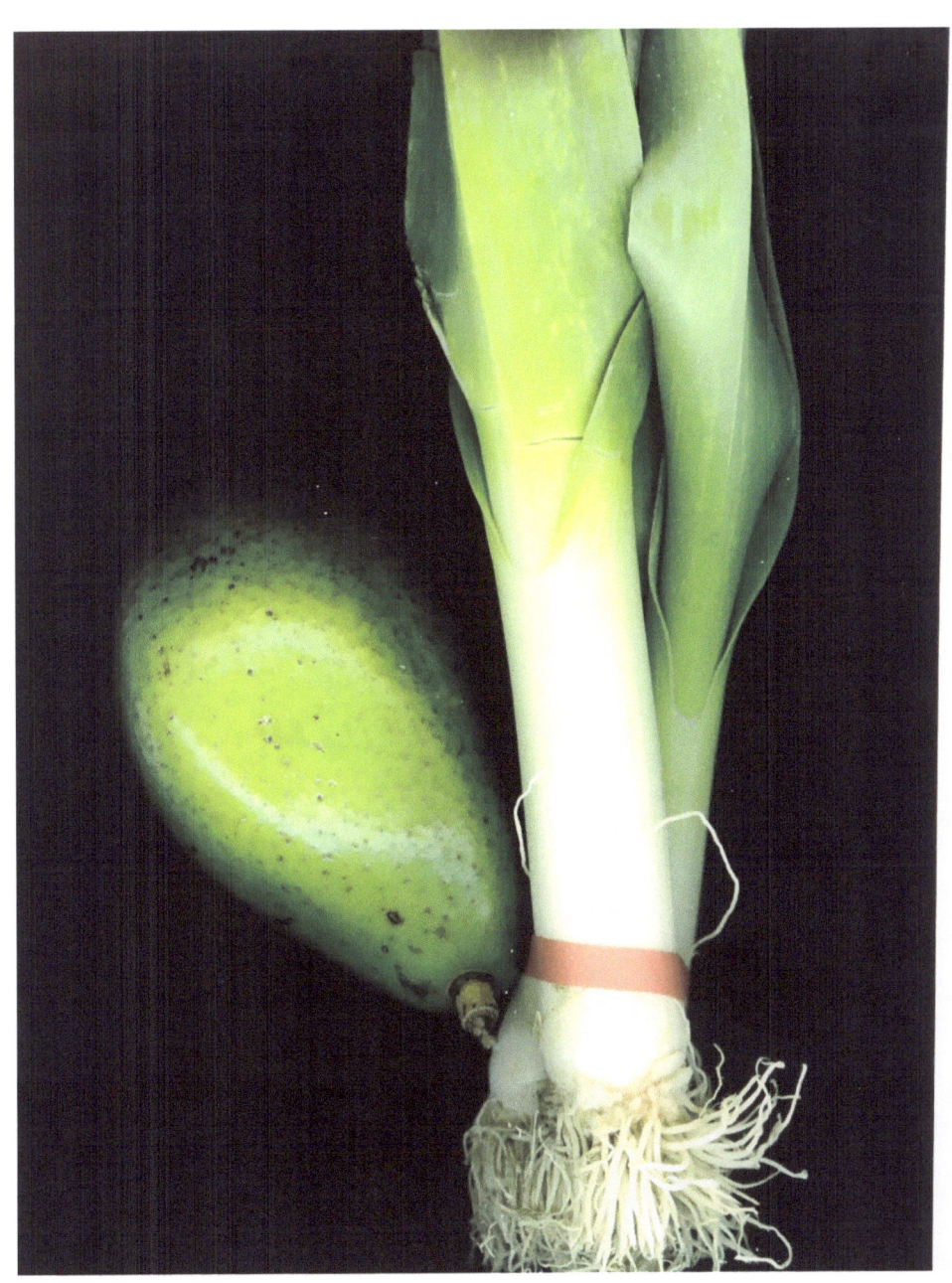

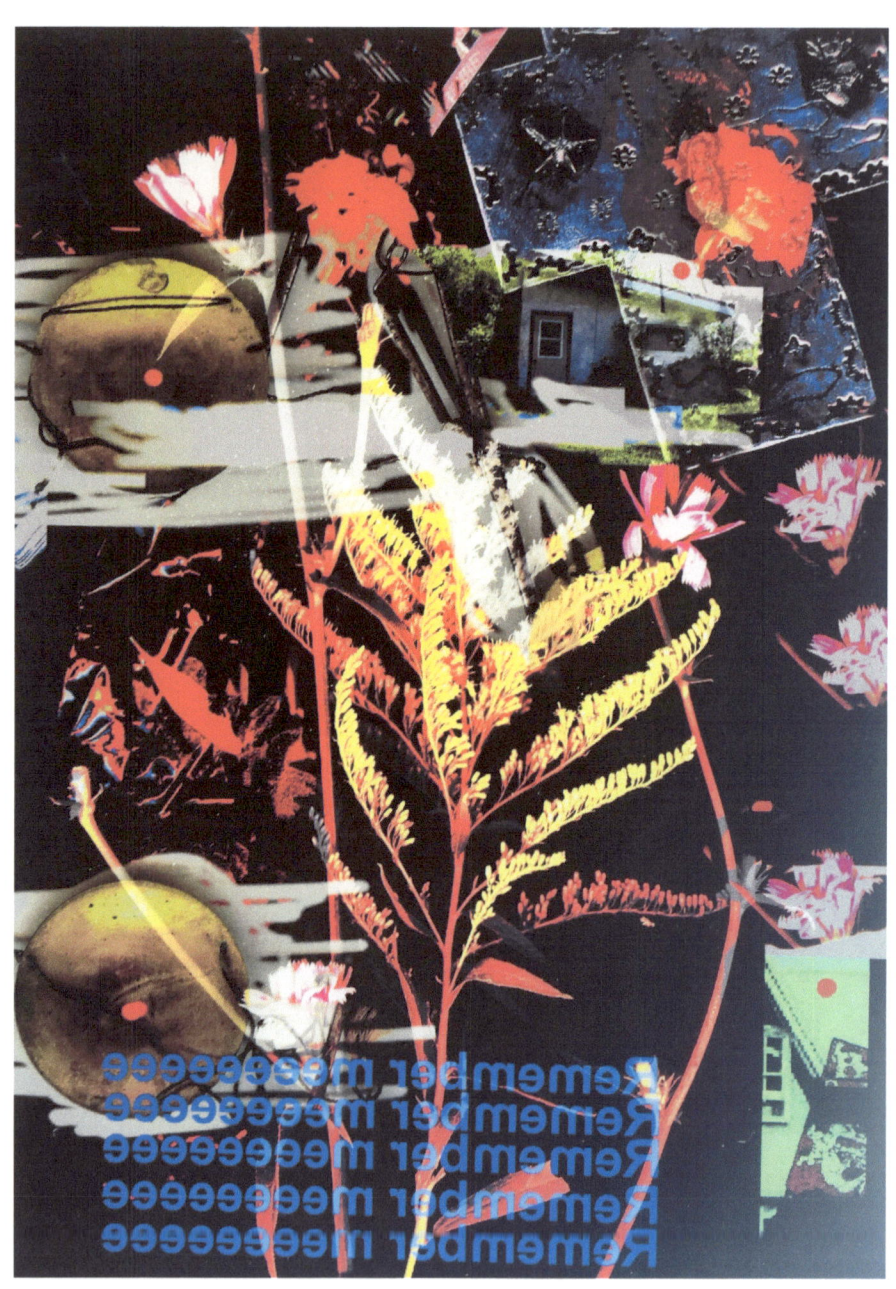

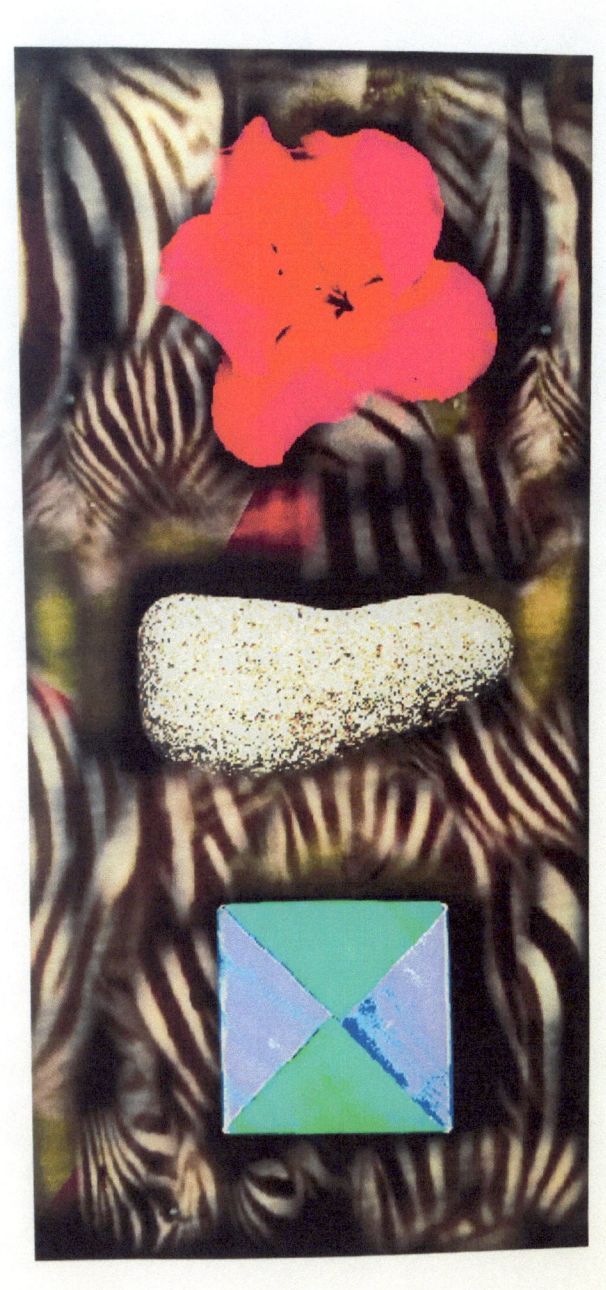

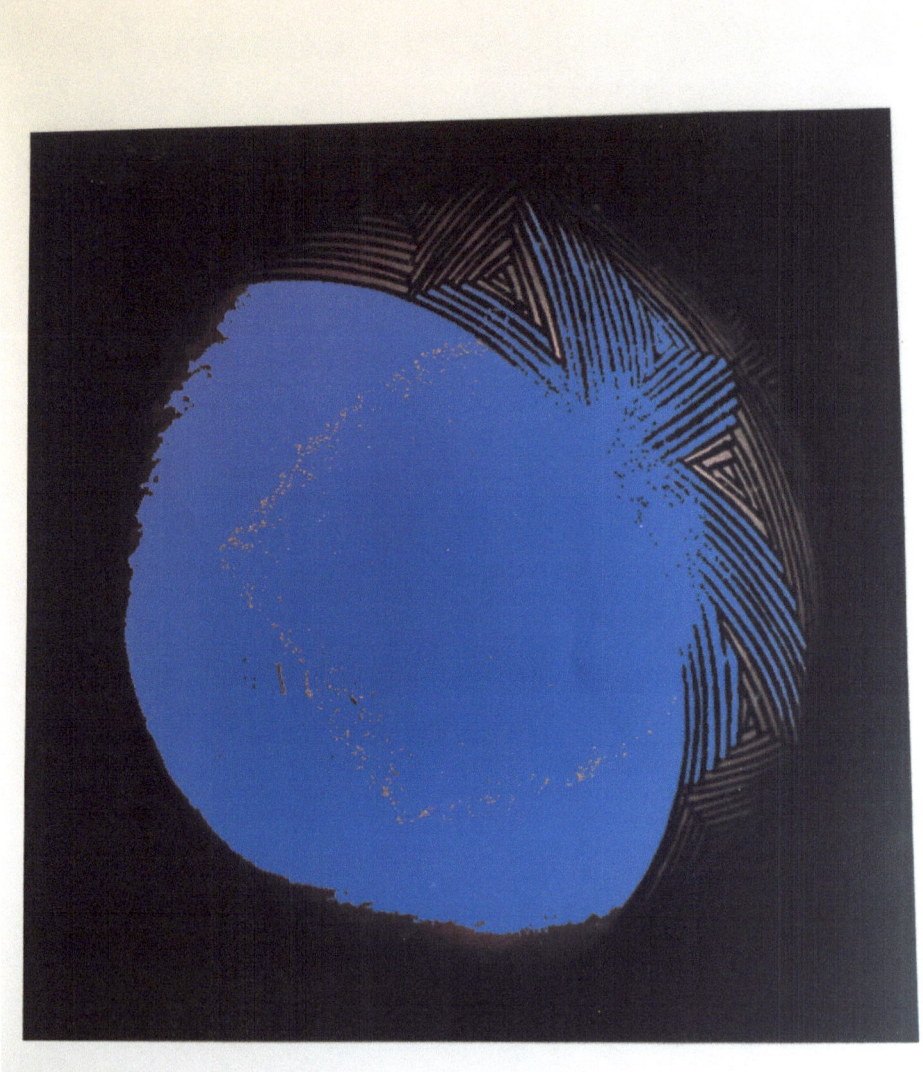

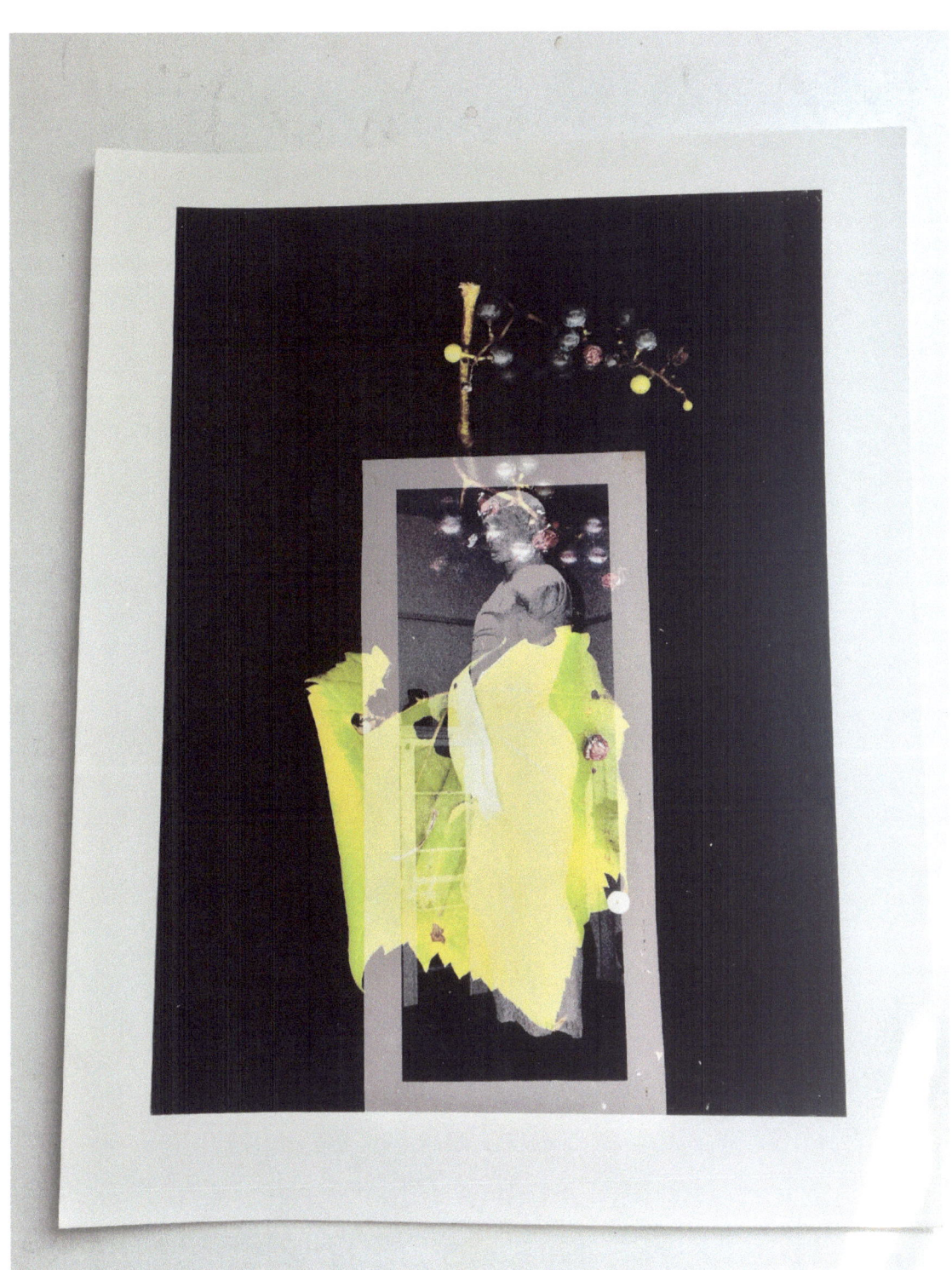

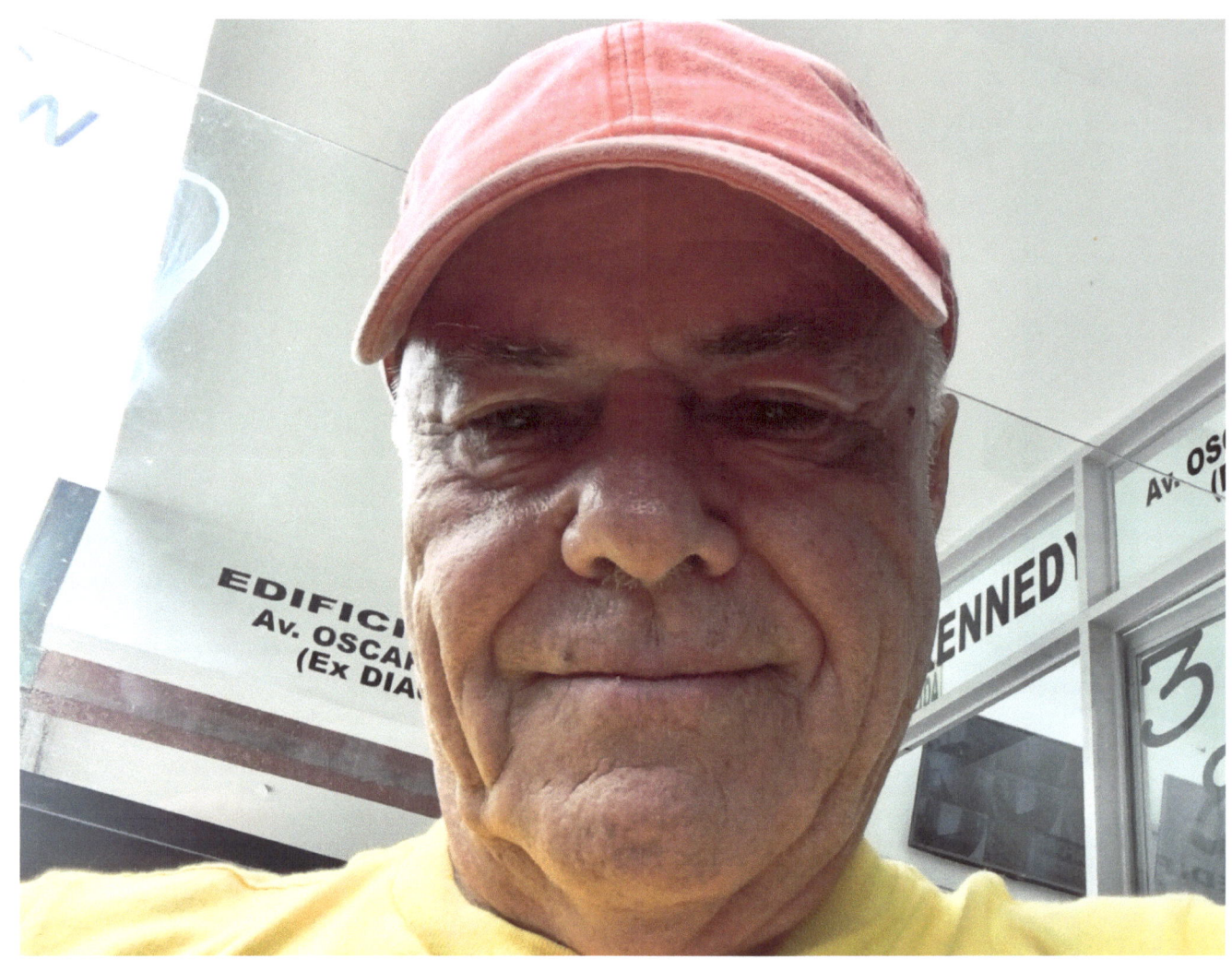

Gary Walters has B.A., M.F.A, and PH.D. degrees
From Princeton University in Romance languages
And the history of art and architecture.
He has taught at McGill and Concordia Universities.
At the latter he was Director of Graduate Studies in
Fine Arts.
He is a practicing artist with some 25 years of
experience and a poet.

He was a visiting lecturer at the University for the Arts in Denpasar, Bali, Indonesia.
He currently lives in Peterborough, Ontario.

www.ingramcontent.com/pod-product-compliance
Lightning Source LLC
Chambersburg PA
CBHW051210220526
45473CB00003B/972